A Year of
Dancing
Dangerously

A Year of Dancing Dangerously

ONE WOMAN'S JOURNEY FROM BEGINNER TO WINNER

Lydia Raurell

Photography by Robert Forbes

OVERLOOK DUCKWORTH
NEW YORK • WOODSTOCK • LONDON

First published in 2008 by
Overlook Duckworth, Peter Mayer Publishers, Inc.
New York, Woodstock, and London

NEW YORK:
141 Wooster Street
New York, NY 10012

WOODSTOCK:
One Overlook Drive
Woodstock, NY 12498
www.overlookpress.com
[for individual orders, bulk and special sales, contact our Woodstock office]

LONDON:
90-93 Cowcross Street
London EC1M 6BF
inquiries@duckworth-publishers.co.uk
www.ducknet.co.uk

Cataloging-in-Publication Data is available from the Library of Congress

The author will be donating a portion of her royalties to charity.

Book design and type formatting by Bernard Schleifer
Manufactured in China
ISBN 978-1-59020-127-5 US
10 9 8 7 6 5 4 3 2 1

To my husband, Bob, my dance partner forever

And a very special thanks to Jeff

To everything there is a season,

and a time to every purpose under the heaven:

A time to be born, and a time to die;

a time to plant, and a time to pluck up that which is planted;

A time to kill, and a time to heal; a time to break down, and a time to build up;

A time to weep, and a time to laugh; a time to mourn, and a time to dance.

—Ecclesiastes 3:1-4

Contents

Introduction   *11*

1: "Walk in Monday, Dance Out Friday"   *21*

2: Wings on My Feet   *33*

3: Sequins and Stockings   *49*

4: First Time Showtime   *59*

5: Getting into the Competition Swing   *67*

6: On the Road   *89*

7: Partnership   *117*

8: The Disipline of the Dance World   *133*

9: Eyes on the Prize   *145*

Acknowledgments   *153*

National Council of America Dance Competitions   *155*

Introduction

BELIEVE ME—DREAMS DO COME TRUE.

On the morning I saw a little dance studio ad in my local paper, I was fifty-four years old. I had been married, a single mother, and married again. I had moved into nine different houses and worked, nonstop, since I was eighteen years old. The death of loved ones, partings from friends and communities, grief, fear, and illness had woven deep lines in my face. I had earned my wrinkles. Change had been forced on me and had become my way of life, but what never changed through it all was my desire to dance.

I knew somewhere in the depths of my heart that I had wanted to dance for a long time, but I had so many commitments to so many people, so many details to look after, that for more than twenty years I kept telling myself the time wasn't right.

There is a magnet on the door of my refrigerator that says *Don't postpone joy.* I guess the morning I stumbled across the Caruso Dancesport Center ad, I finally decided to stop ignoring my magnet. This is the story about how deciding not to postpone my joy changed my life.

I'm sharing my experience in hopes that it might help other women like me who are seeking to rediscover themselves. There are many of us who are eventually forced to confront the question of who we are, and who we want to become. We have made the choice to be caretakers, to provide for our families, whom we cherish, to work at our careers as best we can. This in itself is a huge achievement, but there are dreams that weave their way through our daily lives, filaments of desire and magic, which we put aside in the immediacy of our many obligations.

If we look very closely at the tapestry of our lives, we will find there is always a thread that glimmers, leading to some particular twinkling star. That star is our heart's desire. Dancing was that star for me, that path I had never truly taken. Once I decided to step out, into my dream, it was the beginning of a truly daring adventure.

Dancing gave me even greater faith, confidence, and joy in my daily life. I have very good reason to believe that many other women will find that it may be the key to their own shining star—happiness.

There is always danger when you dare to make your dream into a reality. Most of us are secretly comfortable with letting our dreams remain in a private and comforting fantasy land of make believe. If you decide to live your fantasy you may lose your sense of sanctuary, or even of hope. But if you don't try—well, you will never know if you could actually be that person you imagine.

To face the reality of your dream is to face yourself, in the most profound sense. In confronting all your fears of inadequacy, incompetence, undeservingness, can you bear the possibility of smashing the dream?

Can you bear failure? These are the questions I asked myself, and I knew my desire to dance was so powerful that I would risk it.

To try to fulfill a dream can mean to risk everything—your health, your family, your friends, your finances, and ultimately your own image of who you are. You have to embrace the risk, you literally have to jump off an emotional cliff and go into free fall.

This, then, is the story of my year of discovering competitive ballroom dancing and what it meant to me. It is about setting a tremendous goal to be reached in a year's time. It is about pushing myself to go for it.

I don't think I could have dared without the support of my husband. Without him it would have felt too lonely. But I have always felt that the hardest battles, those we fight at 4 in the morning, are solitary, with no awards and no applause. These are the battles that go on within our psyche, of the self divided between wishing and doing. Will you dare to compete against yourself?

I knew there were no magic wands to make me an instant Dancer. The wand was hours and hours and hours of just plain hard work.

There were moments, even weeks of genuine terror and despair for me. When my mind or my body refused to function at all, much less at the standard I had set, it was truly discouraging. When I had practiced and practiced until I was tired to the bone, and still had not met my expectations, it was agonizing. But I had taken a do-or-die dictum. I was going to give every breath in my body and every shred of will power to make this dream come true. If I failed, or even died in the process, so be it. I would not capitulate.

I was going to dance.

My image of myself as an ill person had to be overcome. I had had years of pain management. I knew what the rules were in order for me to live a normal life. They were a strict regimen of diet, rest, exercise, and minimum stress. The fact that I also had a torn meniscus in both knees, only 50% use of my right arm from a fracture that never healed properly, and damaged nerve roots in my lower back were minor obstacles compared to the pain, and fear of pain, of my stomach syndrome. These were fears I had to get over to achieve my dream of being a serious ballroom competitor. It took all my courage and more. It took every ounce of will power and discipline that I could muster. It was worth it—the music made it worth it, the dancing made it worth everything. It became my life. A healthy life!

Humans are designed to dance. Dance has been part of every culture for thousands of years. Why? Because all of us (and don't tell me you are unmusical!) have rhythm in our very blood, by the simple fact that we have a heartbeat. It is only natural that our bodies respond in movement to the rhythms around us.

There is great physical pleasure in movement, like spinning—it is something we discover as children and never relinquish, although we may become shy to indulge this pleasure. Over many centuries and in many incarnations, dancing has been a form of exercise and artistic expression, of religious ritual, entertainment, culture, and courtship. Because of this, dance has become a sport of joyous celebration, a companionable activity we perform with others at our happiest and most sacred moments. Dance is also one of the few social activities that make use of our whole bodies.

That said, not everyone realizes how much pleasure they might derive from dancing. Sedentary modern culture does not much help us take advantage of our wonderful bodies. Most cultural influences teach

us to hate our bodies and try to change them instead of learning to take joy in the amazing things they can do.

As any woman reading this knows—and, unfortunately, as most men probably know, too—most of us have some kind of heartbreaking love-hate push-pull relationship with our bodies, for some reason or another. The media tells us we're not beautiful or perfect enough, that there is only one kind of beauty and that any deviation from it is a fault.

Ballroom dancing, however, is a great equalizer. Among dancers, physique doesn't matter. Your shape and size are irrelevant, as are how muscular or coordinated you are when you first start to practice. Dancing changes your psychology, filling you with adrenalin, helping you discover the wonder of your body, teaching you muscle control and memory so that your limbs do things you never imagined they'd be able to do. It makes you fitter, healthier and more toned, helping you balance better and be less clumsy. Balance comes with muscle strength, and muscle strength comes quickly as you practice—twenty minutes of Viennese Waltz three times a week is the most efficient aerobic workout you can do.

Dancing radically alters your self-image, invariably making you look and feel healthier and more vibrant. It is an old truism that dancers don't seem to age—and it's true. As you dance, you literally become a work of art, your own masterpiece. You come to love your sport and love what your body does, and soon you find yourself loving that same physical you that you see in the mirror.

Ballroom dancers are computer technicians, health care professionals, teachers, janitors, lawyers, engineers, housewives, receptionists, mothers. We work long hours all week in the office or home, and those weeknights when we come into the studio to dance are our chance to

let magic happen in our daily lives. We go to practice—increasingly, studios and community organizations are popping up all across the country. Sometimes we are there with our spouses, partners, or friends; sometimes we come alone in hopes that we'll meet other people with our similar passion.

I, like other baby boomers, learned to dance during adolescence. We were the generation who invented dancing without a partner. Such monosyllabic dances like the Twist, the Fish, and the Jerk, requiring only the pelvis and arms to move, were products of the 1960s, and they were wildly popular. Later came the Mashed Potato, which had foot work as well as pelvic thrusts, and my favorite, the Motown Boogaloo, which used every part of one's torso and upper body, each going in different directions—a genuine exercise in coordination and what would now be called "isolation" of movement. The only social arena that required partner dancing was weddings.

Thus the tradition of ballroom dancing seemed to fade in the second half of the twentieth century. Thankfully—and what a big thanks I give for it—pop culture has created a true renaissance of ballroom dancing with such movies as *Dirty Dancing* (starring Patrick Swayze), *Shall We Dance* (starring Richard Gere), *Take the Lead* (starring Antonio Banderas), *Strictly Ballroom* (directed by Baz Luhrmann), and *Mad Hot Ballroom* (which features New York public junior high school students who learn competitive ballroom). These films hit the public consciousness like an explosion. Women viewers *really* liked Patrick Swayze, Richard Gere, and Antonio Banderas, and male viewers felt that if those dudes could get out and dance, so could they.

What good impact Hollywood had on ballroom dance was compounded exponentially when reality TV caught wind of the ballroom trend. When the TV series "Dancing with the Stars" and "So You Think You Can Dance?" arrived on the scene, there was an unprecedented growth in the ballroom dance industry, in the United States and abroad. "Ballroom" is now a household word. Over the past four years, these shows have inspired people of all ages to try out this athletic, beautiful, and truly enjoyable sport.

One of the dance judges told me that before these shows came out, he was reluctant to tell people what he did for a living. He'd found that he would often get a suspicious or dubious response. Now everyone he meets is impressed and wants to ask a million questions.

Wonderfully for the many women who have taken up ballroom dancing, these films and TV shows have also inspired many men to start dancing. When I began my ballroom journey in 2004, about ten percent of the competitors were men. Now, four short years later, I am frequently dancing in crowded heats where fifteen to thirty percent of the competitors are male. This renaissance is a happy one both for the sport and for all the women who have had to share dancing partners up until now.

As ballroom dance has become so popular, there are new ballroom dance studios opening up almost every month. In them there is "social dancing," which is a great venue for a beginner to get a taste of the sport. You can go with a partner, with a friend, or by yourself—these studios are always warm, friendly places, and most offer complimentary first lessons for newcomers. Almost all studios will have group classes, which are cheaper (and, for some, less intimidating) than private lessons.

The Yellow Pages are a good place to start your search. You can also look online at *www.dancedirectory.com* or *accessdance.com*, which will give you the names of instructors and studios across the entire country and even the world. Franchise studios like Fred Astaire or Arthur Murray as

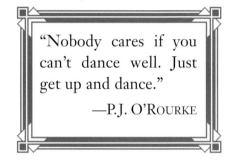

"Nobody cares if you can't dance well. Just get up and dance."
—P.J. O'ROURKE

well as independent studios are excellent. Proximity is a good thing to think about, since a studio nearby will help you easily fit dancing into your work, family, and other commitments—unless you are sick of your own neighborhood, in which case go as far as your gas bill will take you!

Remember when you're starting to check out studios that the teacher is a salesperson who is trained to get you to sign up for a package. It's his or her job. But you are the one who is paying, so start small and then build up if you like it. You should also make sure before you commit to any studio that the chemistry is right for you. The teacher should be clean and well spoken. If he or she talks without directing any movement for more than twenty minutes of a forty-five minute class, try another teacher.

I was reluctant to write this book, since writing a book is a scary enterprise itself, at least as exhibitionistic as getting up in a tiny dress in front of a team of judges and asking them to scrutinize my every move. But my husband, who has been my greatest cheerleader and best friend through this whole adventure, reminded me that dancing had changed my life. "Write the book, Lydia," he said. "It might be what inspires other people to dance, too."

Here I am with Angelo Caruso,
my ballroom teacher and partner,
at out first comp.

Chapter 1

"WALK IN MONDAY, DANCE OUT FRIDAY"

THE AD IN MY LOCAL PAPER WAS SMALL AND UNASSUMING, BUT whoever had placed the ad had been very clever with their words. "Walk in Monday, dance out Friday," it read. This struck me as somehow funny and serious at the same time, its optimism both appealing and manageable.

The truth is, although I was very unsure on my feet the Monday I walked into Caruso Dancesport Palm Beach, I was already deep into a passionate and tumultuous affair with dancing. I think most girls must fantasize about being a dancer at some point in their lives. I, for one, had been carrying around that dream secretly for half a century without ever making good on it.

I had had three previous opportunities to become a dancer, once as a child, once in my late twenties, and once in my early thirties. For a variety of reasons, I let these chances pass me by. I didn't know at the time that another opportunity wouldn't come knocking until I was fifty-four years old.

*Warming up on
a dance floor.*

I have always adored ballet. At age seven I first decided I wanted to be a dancer—a fairy ballerina, like many little girls. It was a huge honor for me to be chosen to perform in the children's Corps de Ballet for several big performances, even more so because I was put in the prima position facing the audience. Sadly, after two years my dance instructor told my mother that my bone structure was too delicate to go onto *pointe*. He said that my ankles were much too fragile to be able to withstand the rigors of full *pointe*.

I was devastated. The memory of my mother's voice, telling me that there would be no more dance lessons, makes me wince to this day. If my parents had been more "stage parents" and less concerned about my health and growth, they might have found another ballet instructor. Or perhaps that was their way of being kind, and I wasn't good enough. Who knows? I don't believe in worrying about "might have beens," but I do know that my first dream of becoming a professional dancer had been squashed, at a tender age.

I didn't return to any kind of formal dance studio until Fate hit me with a big whack when I was in my late twenties. I had gotten married when I was nineteen and had my son when I was twenty-one. Traumatic events in my personal life erupted and I found myself a single mother, working two jobs just to make ends meet. One of these was clerical work, which I did from 9 to 2 without a lunch break. That way I could have time to pick up my son from school and be with him in the afternoon.

I also worked as a freelance "slush pile" reader, evaluating unsolicited manuscripts for a number of publishing houses, reading a minimum of ten books a week, and writing a précis and recommendation for each. Literature had always been an integral part of my life, so this wasn't too

Dancing at my first comp.

difficult for me as a second job I could do at home. As many fulltime parents know, there isn't much time for extra anything after work and making a home. Homes are sacred places, small or large, rich or poor, and they need much care to become so.

As luck would have it, my health began to deteriorate and I developed a chronic stomach condition that required frequent medical visits and medications. My life reorganized itself around pain management. I still dreamed of dancing, and would watch ballet on PBS, and every Fred Astaire movie I could find. My babysitter came once a week, on Saturday afternoons, to give me a little freedom. One afternoon during my errands I saw a studio that was advertising Tango lessons, with the first lesson free. The next Saturday I went with an old friend of mine, a physicist, to take a lesson in the Tango. Neither of us could afford anything extra, but we did meet the "TangoMaster," our teacher, a short, stocky, forty-year-old guy who spent the next forty minutes quietly luring us to the wild shores the very emotional Tango.

> The human body is designed to take great pleasure in movement. I have always known how much I adored to dance. It is one of the special activities that allows you to move every muscle in your body.

TANGO

Everyone knows about the Tango, the famous wild dance of passion and jealousy. The Tango is one of the most fascinating dances in the ballroom repertoire because of the elaborate story it tells, and because of the violent and poetic ways it has fused the musical cultures and histories of so many countries. It is an urban dance, originally done on concrete or pavement or in the back alleys of Argentina, danced to vibrant music inspired by various European heritages. It quickly became popular in theatres or on the street with barrel organs playing, making it a favorite among working people. Since it is such a naturally competitive dance—in the Tango, the man and woman are almost competing against each other!—it quickly evolved into a fiery, challenging showpiece for couples in one of the earliest and most organic forms of competitive ballroom.

The Tango came easily to me. It is fierce and predatory, and this is the only dance in which it is not appropriate to smile. The steps are catlike, precise and discrete, with your knees flexed nearly the entire dance. The difficulty I have in this dance is that I tend to "backlead" (that is, I get so into the music that I start going much faster than my partner, thus I am leading and not letting him lead—this is very bad). The ballroom Tango is very different from the Argentine Tango, but the wild energy and urban flair found in them is the same. I particularly like the Tango because I am allowed to do mini-drops like the *corté*.

When the Tango is danced badly, nothing looks worse—think of all those horrible movies with Englishmen clomping across the floor with straight arms and a rose in their teeth. The trick is to make the story of the dance *believable*. Angelo and I growl at each other when we are doing the Tango, to make it easier to get in the mode. I have to be squished up to Angelo as though we were connected by Velcro. It is actually hilarious to practice because there are many bumps and lurches before you can reach this connection.

...ngelo and I practice the Tango
...our warm-up gear.

That was the first time I ever tipped my toe into the magnetic river of ballroom dancing, and I was touched forever. I *knew* that this was something I would do—not then, maybe not for years, as I had raising my son, the biggest challenge of my life, to complete before I could take that kind of time for myself. Devoting this part of my life to him was one of the happiest choices I've made. My heart was with him and that was what mattered most. Fate and free will are joined. Fate offers us events—free will is how we respond to those events.

Ten years later I found myself taking ballroom dance group classes at the same studio where the TangoMaster used to work. He had moved on but another teacher had taken over that tiny space and the big studio next door. Life had given me a big kiss in my second marriage to the dearest man in the world, Bob. The poor guy must had been shot by Cupid, and after four years of courtship we were very happily married. This was almost a miracle for me—I had never expected that such deep love could come to me, and my daily prayers were bright and happy.

A wonderful friend had told me I should go back to college to finish my degree and she would lend me the money to do so! I had never borrowed funds before in my life, but I accepted and spent the next fifteen years studying part time to obtain my degree from Columbia University. I was still working and parenting and now making a home for three. It was a busy, blossoming time, full of love and energy.

Then another big slap hit me, the event I now call my Big Challenge. Death came to someone very dear to me and I found myself in serious need of solace. We all have our personal therapies, and this time, I knew that in order to get out of that pit of grief, my therapy had to include dance.

So, there I was, remarried, taking private lessons with my husband for one hour once a month, and taking group classes once a week by myself. I was in the very beginner section, learning how to make a box, a right turn and a left. I knew some of the rudiments already—that posture was important, that a waltz was based on a three-count. There were seven different teachers and each one had their own habits and style, so I was introduced to many of the various facets of ballroom.

I let my new hobby dispell my grief. Dancing was all I wanted to do, and I became sort of possessed for nearly a year. The rest of my life started to fade, the sound of the music and the steps in the ballroom were my escape from sadness. But at the end of that year, I realized that my life was out of balance. My true desire was with to be with my family, my studies, and my work. This was *not* my time to dance, so I stopped.

Twenty danceless years later, I saw that fateful ad in my local paper. My circumstances had changed immensely in the interim. My son was grown up. I owned a home and had three secure years without any mortgage payments. I had a loving family around me, and a husband who wanted me to fulfill my passion in life. I had friends in my community and a solid, stable job I loved at an international magazine. I was fifty-four years old, and after many years of focusing on others, I was ready to discover myself again.

That was why when I idly flipped through the *Shiny Sheet*, the local newspaper on that balmy weekend, my eye stalled for an unusually long time on Angelo's ad. Something clicked in my brain. *Why not?*

Dancing had been my precious dream for over twenty years, so my wish to become a dancer had retreated into a distant star in my mental topography. Quite honestly, I think I had almost buried it in that impossible realm of "some day when the time is right." At a certain season in our lives we realize that our time may be running out. For me,

After a long set of heats, we pu
our warm-up jackets and a
award results. In the cold
room, the jackets keep us f
getting too s

at that moment, I realized there could be no more waiting. The conditions were perfect; the studio was five minutes from my house and the first lesson was free. What did I have to lose?

That was the day I called and made an appointment for my introductory lesson with Angelo Caruso, the studio owner and teacher who would end up reshaping my life.

His studio is up a flight of steep, dark stairs. The stairs, I later learned, are a kind of hazing process—you have to be able to get up them if you want to be able to dance, according to Angelo. The studio is inviting, about a thousand feet square, with polished hardwood floors. It is naturally lit, with windows that open on two sides. This is probably part of the reason the studio is so intimate, since having light coming in from two sides doubles poor Angelo's rent, but it's important to him to have fresh air circulating. Everything is spotless, and the wood floor is the kind that springs back against your step.

Angelo Caruso is a truly extraordinary man. He is polite and well-spoken and has the physique of a football player. The first time we met, I asked him to disco with me—a very obnoxious request on my part. He complied, and told me that in the ballroom dance world, this type of dancing is known as freestyle, not disco. At first I thought he was a little stiff, but soon I realized he has more rhythm in any single cell in his body than any other human I have ever met. To my utter delight, he made me laugh even during my first nervous meeting with him. That moment was the beginning of our partnership. Without humor, there is no joy, and without joy, you cannot truly dance.

Angelo is half-German, half-Italian, an all-American Jersey boy with a quick tongue and a heart of gold. He was only twenty years old when he first went to Hollywood to try to make his way as an actor and comedian—and let me tell you, this man is funny. It was by accident that he found dance, his true calling.

Angelo, you see, was also a single parent, just like I had been. He took up a job teaching ballroom dance at Arthur Murray to support his family and now has twenty years of championship-level instruction under his belt. He is again happily married, with two children, two step-children, and two step-grandchildren.

The fact that he has been a single parent is manifest in his teaching style. He very consciously cares for other people, always attentive to the tiniest details in my carriage, eyes constantly roaming the floor to plot our path through the other weaving couples. He takes the responsibility of leading his partner very seriously, which is an immense relief to a beginner like I was. His deft and expert direction lets me focus on my steps, my posture, the angles of my limbs. This is why all of his students blossom under his tutelage.

Destiny, I believe, interceded more than once on Angelo's behalf to make sure he was perfectly suited to become a dance teacher. For example, he grew up with five sisters. "There's nothing about women I don't know," he'll tell you, and, as I've learned, he means it. There is no mystique—Angelo knows exactly how many hairpins are digging into my scalp before a performance, how much my feet hurt from wearing high heels for hours on end, how frustrating make-up application can be, especially when you are trying to get it done at 6 o'clock in the morning. Angelo understands that I, like almost every woman on the planet, have some body issues that erode my self-confidence periodically, and he knows all the right things to say to remind me how beautiful I am, how glamorous we all become when we let ourselves become part of the dance. Angelo is very aware of beauty. "I'm more vain than any woman,"

he says, laughing. He loves clothes, and he loves to go shopping. He has to look snappy for all his clients. Most dance instructors love fashion, and all have their own personal style. Since they have an innate sense of the "showbiz" aspect of ballroom dance, many of them choose their students' dresses as well.

He is completely at ease with me and his other female students. There was never a sense of awkwardness at having to be physically close to a strange man when I first began to dance with him. In fact, Angelo sneakily coaxed me into absolute physical comfort around him without my even noticing. I was, as I think many people are when they first start partner dancing, nervous about moving around in such close proximity to another person, one whom I did not know. During our first private lesson, Angelo made his supporting arms into a careful and perfect cage, keeping me comfortably at arm's length and watching me with his wise, appraising eye. Three months later, I was dancing against his shoulder as comfortably as any couple you might see in a movie or on TV. I never noticed the transition—he actually had to point it out to me. "I've inched you closer over the last twelve weeks," he told me. "I needed you to get close eventually, but I wanted to make sure that you never felt out of your comfort zone. This is how I can tell you trust me as a partner."

Most extraordinarily, Angelo is partially deaf. His parents first discovered this when he was only four years old, so he has had his entire life to acclimate himself, but it is nonetheless remarkable that he has made his livelihood out of music—and made it well. He wears a hearing aide in one ear, but when he takes it out he can hear nothing. He is a prizewinning dancer and instructor despite this handicap, which other

Angelo leads me in one of my first ever competive dance heats, in one of my first dresses at my very first comp.

less courageous souls might imagine to be a debilitating one. His technique is so magnificent that is overrides the fact that he often starts a measure later than the other dancers. He is always on the beat, but must often wait to make sure he can hear it properly.

Perhaps it his acutely developed visual understanding of the world that has made him as adept a teacher as he is. He misses nothing—nothing. Not a hair out of place, a hanging sequin, a threading hem. His eye for precision angles has helped me refine my balance, coordination, and limb positions in ways I never would have thought possible a few years ago. He is a perfect teacher because he lets absolutely no mistake slip past him during practice. I know when I go before judges to compete that not one of those judges will monitor me as carefully as Angelo has during practice. In a way, the pressure's off. He's prepared me for everything.

The fact that in his life he has to rely so heavily on his vision makes him a consummate navigator, as well. Dance floors are frequently packed at competitions, with dozens of couples jamming the floor, all somehow trying to move elegantly and freely. Although a couple will know its own dance routine inside and out, there is, of course, no way to guarantee that one couple's choreography will work out geographically with that of any of the other couples on the floor, never mind that of *all* the couples. As a result, it is imperative that a dance team have a strong leader with a sharp sense of timing, depth, and distance.

Angelo Cha-Chas his way through those couples like a big sweaty cat—he is never caught without the perfect hairsbreadth of space. I have wondered in the past if he doesn't have some kind of invisible whiskers that let him be the perfect judge of where we need to go at what exact moment and how we're going to get there. I have enough to think about with all my steps (which are, naturally, newer to me than they are to

Angelo, but still). Angelo, on the other hand, can see the entire dance floor like a chessboard, scanning the floor to position us for our choreography. Not only does he know where each couple is right now, he is able to intuit where precisely they will be in half a second, two seconds, eight seconds. It is, in my eyes, miraculous.

All teachers, however, must be able to navigate around the floor. This skill is called "floor craft," and some couples are able to swoop in and around the other dancers like swallows. This level of technique is a wonder to behold. A couple's ability to dance like that is a definite sign of good partnership, as the female dancer must always carry fifty percent of the responsibility for these complex maneuvers. If I see another couple barreling down on us from behind Angelo, I will try to direct him away or to pause by gently squeezing his arm. Trying to stop Angelo requires a lot of pressure in my arm squeeze, which is a real trick for me to do while maintaining my frame. This is the same secret communication we use when I am responsible for finding "clearance"—that is, an opening between all the couples so we can fly down the floor.

Needless to say, my first sample lesson with Angelo was not my last. I left his studio that first day having signed up for a whole regimen of classes. I was on my way to becoming a dancer. At last, I was turning my dream into a reality.

*T*o enter the world of competitive ballroom dancing is to enter a foreign country. It is a place of rigorous order, with its own traditions, rituals, hierarchy, and language. It has its own music, its own dress code and its own unique aesthetic. It is a world where every step you take is codified, scripted, and predetermined.

Like the foreign country it is, ballroom dance has its own foreign language. The required dance steps have their own vocabulary in the same way that ballet has its own vocabulary—or, for that matter, the same way that football has *its* own vocabulary. The language, or syllabi, can vary according to the level and category of dance. The syllabi are determined by the organizations that regulate and administrate competitive ballroom.

You start with the basics, as with any language. There are the four basic positions of your feet, which are like the vowels of the dancing language; the steps you take, which are like the syllables; the sequences of steps, which are the sentences; and finally the paragraphs: fully choreographed sets of sequential steps.

Every dance step has a name—for example, there is the Box Step, the Under Arm Turn, and the Hesitation, just to name a few basics—and all of these have to be memorized both verbally and physically. As you

llroom dance originated as a socially
ceptable form of courtship, and much of
t formality and pageantry survives in
dern competitive ballroom. In these three
tos we have Preparation, Approaching,
d finally Connection for the Waltz. All this
takes place before we take our first dance
p, but it is part of the prescribed ritual and
st be executed correctly.

progress as a student, new steps are added to your repertoire, according to your ability and the syllabus. The dance vocabulary becomes more complex as you learn, for example, the Chassé, Tipple, Whisk, Cuddle, Betty Boop, Attitude (yes, that's a dance step!) and New Yorker.

SOME DANCE STEPS

Box	"Around the World"
Turning Right Box	Sliding Doors
Turning Left Box	Explosion
Under Arm Turn	Attitude
Hesitation	New Yorker
Chassé	Heel Pull
Tipple	Telemark
Whisk	Slip Pivot
Rondé	Pivot
Developé	Cross Body Lead
Cuddle	5th Position Break
Betty Boop	Half-Moon
Windows	Crossover
	Double Reverse

I dance twenty-five different dances, in all four categories of ballroom. This means I have had to learn approximately one hundred steps in each of those twenty-five dances, or 2500 new vocabulary words. Talk about exercising your brain!

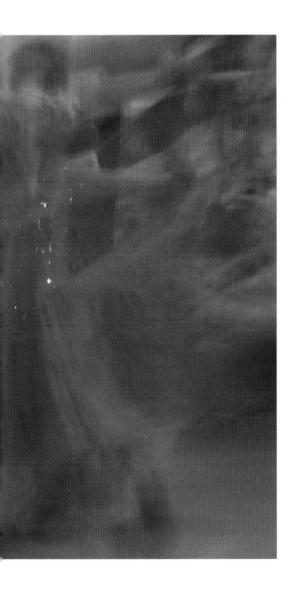

The rule for learning ballroom is that you always start (as with many things in life) feet first. Then you add the arms, then the upper body, then the head. All of these movements of every part of the body also have a name. If you add up that vocabulary, you're clocking in approximately 3500 words.

Ideally, you should know each of the steps without your partner, meaning you should be able to do them solo. The key to ballroom dance is to then be able to perform these steps with a partner, in the dance frame.

There are a number of ballroom divisions with different regulations, depending on where you compete and what dances you compete in. Since I learned to dance and compete in the United States, I started off learning American Smooth and American Rhythm.

AMERICAN SMOOTH

Foxtrot
Tango
Waltz
Viennese Waltz
Peabody

AMERICAN RHYTHM

Cha Cha	Mambo
Rumba	Hustle
East Coast Swing	Merengue
West Coast Swing	Samba
Bolero	Salsa

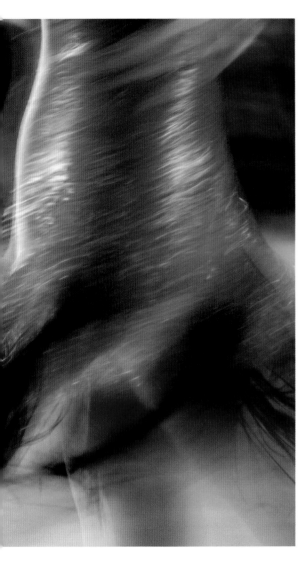

Angelo and I execute the Balancente in the International Samba.

Elsewhere in the world, competitors dance the international equivalents of those two divisions, which are the International Standard and International Latin. Most dancers learn all the different versions of the various dances, although often we specialize and compete only in certain dances. Angelo said I was like a kid in a candy store—I wanted to do all the dances. So I did!

INTERNATIONAL STANDARD

Waltz
Tango
Viennese Waltz
Foxtrot
Quickstep

INTERNATIONAL LATIN

Cha-Cha
Samba
Rumba
Paso Doble
Jive

Each of the twenty-five dances has a unique mood and attitude, its own rhythm, and its own spirit. I like all the dances, since each one lets me act out a different character. Ballroom dance is all about romance, especially courtship, and each dance is an enactment of a different episode in courtship. For example, the waltz character is very lyrical, the story about a couple blissfully floating in love, while the tango character is almost angry, the tumultuous story of jealousies and misunderstood affections.

Because of the courtship pageantry behind all of the dances, I needed to learn to understand my own romance styles and moods. I quickly discovered that I was lousy at playing "sexy," so I learned to opt for flirtation instead. Sexy, it turns out, is a very difficult role to take—it requires physical strength and a lot of power and definitiveness in movement as well as relentless body control. Until I develop that power and control—which, I've realized, will take years—I've decided to play up my grace and femininity when I dance, focusing on appearing elegant, quick, and sweet.

Angelo and I win most often when we dance the Viennese Waltz. My second favorite dance is the Bolero, which I find endlessly fascinating because of the way it combines Rhythm and Smooth elements. It is also a slower Rhythm dance, and I find the slower dances challenging because of the control and expression they require. With the Bolero, as with all dances, I know I have so much more to learn and to practice. I have to learn the "butterfly" aspect, the quality of dancing where some part of my body is always moving, gracefully and in continuity.

The gentleman is always the leader. He initiates what, when, and where you take any given dance step. He also controls the tempo of each step, which must be in accord with the type of dance. As a follower, the

Dancing the Bolero, my favorite of all the dances.

lady must be on hold, waiting for her partner's lead. It is the most intense kind of "listening" your body can do. You must be aware of his every movement, in a constant state of anticipation. This is how partnership is created. Without close listening and anticipation, there is only bumping, staggering, lurching, and, ultimately, chaos.

As with all languages, there is logic to almost all the steps, and how they follow one another. The challenge is to learn the logic mentally and physically, and then to memorize it. If everyone studied ballroom dancing, I can guarantee there would be less Alzheimer's.

When Fred Astaire was asked how he became such a brilliant dancer, he replied, "Practice, practice, practice, and more practice." In the three daily hours of practice, Angelo will choose what dances we work on. Most often he will alternate by category, so one day we will do half American Smooth, half American Rhythm. The following day, we will word on International Standard and International Latin. I wear whatever is comfortable, whatever won't get in the way and is perspiration-friendly. I have "practice" shoes, lace-up low-heeled pumps in a very dreary putty color. I can never find shoes narrow enough for me, so I add white socks. It's quite a look.

Each individual student will find that some dances come more easily than others—who knows why. Some dances feel like I have been born doing them, while others are as difficult as fitting a square peg in a round hole. This is when my obsession really helps get me over the humps. For example, the Mambo was my nemesis.

"Keep your feet *apart*," Angelo would instruct.

So I would tell my feet, "Do what you're supposed to do." My feet would keep touching each other.

"APART!" Angelo would shout. I would watch his feet five times. I would watch them so hard I would bore a hole through them with my eyes. By maybe the 300th try—and this is not an exaggeration—my feet would finally start that *2, 3, 4, hold! 2, 3, 4, hold!* and pass by each other instead of touching. Victory!

MAMBO

The Mambo, the quintessential Rhythm dance based on the Cuban Motion step, is a sultry and sinuous dance out of which grew many of the other great Latin dances (like the Salsa and the Cha-Cha). The Mambo was originally a Cuban dance that became popular in the 1940s with the fusion of swing and local music. The word "Mambo," though, is actually Haitian; it's the word for a voodoo priestess. Sometimes I wish I were one when I'm dancing the Mambo, because sometimes I'm not sure how I'll ever master the Cuban Motion step without a little black magic!

The Cuban Motion and Cuban Walk are dreaded by me, the #2 obstacle of the Rhythm dances (the #1 obstacle being the revealing little dresses I need to wear when I perform them!). The Cuban Motion is a certain transition from bent knee to straight knee, which results in a specific movement of the hips. After years of practice, I've got the Cuban Motion down ok—not great, just ok. But the Cuban Walk still eludes me. I can conjure the speed and the energy, I make my whole mind and mood Cuban, but that walk will probably take me another five more years to learn correctly. Or maybe twenty! But I'll keep plugging away, since all the serious rhythm dances—Rumba, Cha-Cha, Swing, Mambo, Merengue, and Samba—are based on the Cuban Motion.

Don't get me wrong—I love the American Rhythm dances. They are called Rhythm dances because rhythm is what they're all about! They are sensuality, love, seduction, rejection—all primal emotions performed at really fast tempos. These are dances that really rock the room. They are hot!

Angelo quickly realized that it was best to warm me up in the morning by doing a dance I really enjoy: the Hustle. This is the dance that made *Saturday Night Fever* such a hit. Almost everyone can do an imitation of John Travolta's routine, so our mornings start off with disco music.

Angelo will introduce a new dance by playing the music so I can hear what the mood and tempo are. Then he will dance a few bars on his own so I can watch. He turns off the music and teaches me the basic steps. I don't get music again until I have learned the steps.

"*Count!*" he used to say.

"Count what?" I retorted.

"Your feet!"

"There are two!" I answered.

"No, Meatball, count your *feet!*"

By this, I finally figured out, he meant that I had to count every beat of the music with my feet. Every time I change weight on my feet was one count.

"Ok, Turkeyburger," I'd smile back.

Although the many levels of refinement can seem intimidating, it is a fact that anyone can learn to ballroom dance. I once said to a friend that all you need to be able to do to become a dancer is to walk, but then I remembered the groups of talented and gorgeous ballroom dancers who are bound to wheelchairs. If you are blind, you can rely on the music. Dancing is such a natural thing for human beings to do that the only real requirement is that you have a heartbeat.

Ballroom dancing is a fantasy world where all women are princesses—princesses who also happen to have calf muscles of iron.

An Advance Left Turn in the Viennese Waltz.

What is it like to ballroom dance? Your skin tingles, your palms itch as your heart pulses. It feels like ginger-ale bubbling through your capillaries. You can feel your heart knocking against your ribcage. The muscles in your calves spark as they slide against each other and you would give anything, anything, to not weaken and fall short.

Now imagine that you somehow have to do all this while looking beautiful and keeping with the music. Then you will understand ballroom dancing.

Ballroom dancing, you see, is both a sport and an art form. There are a couple of other activities—figure skating, for example, or gymnastics. It is true that there is a lot of poetry to be found in the fine execution of many sports—the careful choreography of players on a soccer field, the powerful lines of a sprinter's muscles. In ballroom dancing, however, a competitor is scored entirely by their artistry, by the elegance and precision of their movements.

Dancing is, however, a very athletic and highly aerobic sport. It is a total body workout, using every muscle, from the tip of your toe to the crown of your head. That crushing feeling of your heart ready to burst inside your chest because you're working so hard? Yes, dancers get that, just like runners.

In the course of a single minute-long heat, our heart rates escalate so that the moment we step off the floor, even Angelo, a seasoned athlete, is panting and heaving like a sled dog (I don't understand why I don't get winded, but I don't). The key phrase being "the moment we step off the floor"—for when you're dancing, no one should be able to detect how hard you are working. That would undermine your artistry, much of

which is centered on suppressing the sense that your body is doing something extraordinary and taxing right now.

As a result, much of a dancer's training involves learning to control your body, control its every tiniest movement. In order to do that, you need to learn about your every joint and muscle. Most of us do not naturally know every fiber of our body. In fact, many of us spend years running away from the realities of our bodies, and because of this, the initial getting-to-know-yourself phase comes as new and strange.

You are learning carriage, confidence, grace, and poise. The simplest of everyday functions—walking down a sidewalk, for example, or sweeping a floor, or hailing a cab—can be commonplace or beautiful. A dancer knows how to imbue the motion with meaning, deliberateness, and appreciation for life. We are wondrous creatures, and we have been given bodies that do remarkable things. When you dance, you come to understand this.

This is why, you'll notice, there are all kinds of competitive dancers who don't conform to fashion media's rules at all, and yet you know when you look at them that they are truly beautiful—and by this I mean, in the conventional sense, visually stunning—people. Learning to dance helps a person learn the components of true beauty and remind their own body of its natural purpose in life: to exist, for a reason.

Dancing makes you deliberate in all your actions, even the most commonplace ones. When you first learn to quickstep, you are worried about those quick steps. As the steps become more natural and routine, your mind goes to the other corners of your body, and you are suddenly aware of things you hadn't thought about before—is your sternum facing the ceiling or the wall? Do you fan your fingers on your partner's arm or keep them aligned? When each tiny detail begins to invade a dancer's consciousness, she develops a habit of walking through her daily life with a vivid intelligence of her own every move. She starts to understand the wonder of space and contours around her. It is a form of enlightenment.

Part of my enlightenment was getting past my own body issues. Mine, I'll admit, are a little unusual. Most American women are taught to think they are too fat. I, on the other hand, am too thin. I am what doctors call an ectomorph, with a muscle and bone structure so narrow it is difficult for me to retain weight or gain muscle mass—a real challenge for an athlete. Just to make it through a full day of competition dancing I have had to train for hours with special exercises for my quads and calves, to make sure my lean build will hold me up.

My body has also rebelled against me in many other ways over the years. It has caused me chronic pain and run me through a ragged list of cures and quick-fixes. I understand now that for many of those years I was warring against my own body, willing it to stop hurting me and just be whole and useful like other bodies seem to be; what it really wanted was to be used deliberately. In the end, the only thing that helps me is exercise, and dancing, as I have said, is one of the best forms of exercise there is.

I grew up in a very strict household, and although I left when I was only seventeen to live on my own, the rigidity of my upbringing still affects me to this day. It did help me a lot in my dancing in that I was used to discipline, rigid schedules, hard work, obedience, and the absolute necessity of getting A's on my report card. One of the hardest parts of dancing for me was letting myself let go, to feel at one with my movements, to smile, and to feel confident.

What really brings together all my love for the movement is the music. Music is the wind that drives the dancer's soul, mind, and body. It is the beginning, middle, and end of every gesture and every nuance. Music is

infinite in its moods and emotions—a dancer tries to become the instrument that the music plays. That is the task, and the miracle, of dance.

Music has always been the river along which my life has flowed: lullabies sung to me as a child, sung again when I became a mother. The sound of the piano, played by my father, and then myself—Bach, Mozart, Vivaldi, and Beethoven were as familiar to me as the clattering rhythm of the old shutters of our house. When I couldn't afford the space or cost of a piano, I taught myself to play the recorder, concentrating on Bach and classical French duets.

Music is everywhere and anywhere. It is the sound of motion moving through air, sound waves, water waves, radio, and iPod. It is the sound of sirens, of vacuum cleaners, of trains and footsteps and subways. There is always music. Music is a language anyone can understand. It is the sound of the universe.

All the music in ballroom dance is about love. At every comp there is a music director whose function is to select and play the music for the dancing. This means he plays a repertoire for three to five days for every category of dance, which, when you add showcases, theatre arts, and the professional shows, comes to over thirty different kinds of dance, each of which requires a specific rhythm. He is the musical maestro, whose day begins at the first heat and ends at the last professional show of the night, which can be as late as one in the morning. Their endurance is simply astonishing.

The range of ballroom music goes from classical instrumental, like Strauss's "Blue Danube Waltz," to George Gershwin, Cole Porter, and Irving Berlin, to melodic singers like Elvis Presley, Peggy Lee, Frank Sinatra, and Aretha Franklin. The music is paramount; it is what tells us what and how to dance. The tempo for the American Waltz is much quicker than the tempo of the International Waltz. The music master knows all this; he is our conductor.

Dancers are taught how to count out our dances with no music. In fact, I think there should be a category of "silent" dancing, where only the internal count is exhibited with no music at all. Then the judges would *really* see who had good footwork and how to dance on phrase.

Dancers are the musical instruments. We "play" the musical notes with our feet and arms and body. Half of the joy of ballroom dancing is the music itself.

We may have had four hours of sleep, woken at 5 AM, rammed our feet into the shoes, and wolfed down a banana, but when we get to the ballroom and hear a heartrending Waltz or a sizzling Cha-Cha, the magic starts. There is only the music, and we, who will try to *become* that music.

During the course of my ballroom education, I made a friend whom I consider to be my mentor. She is eighty-two years old. She's a breast cancer survivor and has had two hip replacements, her husband has Alzheimer's, and yet everyday she juggles all of these incredible pressures and still gracefully manages her dancing. I have learned so much from her, about perseverance, a human's incredible capacity for self-reflection and self-perfection, and about dance technique itself. She is proof to me that not only does practice change us as artists, it lifts us up as people, and offers us hope and inspiration.

CHA-CHA

I say the Cha-Cha sizzles because the energy of the dance ripples, not only across the dance floor but through each individual dancer. Like the other great rhythm dances, it was born out of the Mambo, although the Cha-Cha beat has become very distinctive as the dance has evolved. You can hear in the dance name the way the rhythm shakes through your body—*cha cha cha*, like you are a human maraca. The original name of the dance was, in fact, the Cha-Cha-Cha, since that is the noise a dancer's feet make, *slow-slow-quick-quick-quick*, or *one-two-cha-cha-cha*.

The Cha-Cha is Angelo's favorite, and boy is it amazing the way every single muscle of his body moves so perfectly to music. The Cha-Cha, sadly, is my weakest of the Rhythm dances, which just gives me ever more to aspire toward. Just wait—in a couple more years, I'll be sizzling, too!

Chapter 3
SEQUINS AND STOCKINGS

*B*allroom dance is a particularly aesthetic social skill that grew up as a respectable way for ladies and gentlemen to meet, spend time together, and to court. But as anyone who has ever seen *Shall We Dance?* or "So You Think You Can Dance?" knows, there is a whole world of competitive dancing that isn't about socializing or courtship. It's about winning.

A ballroom dance competition—"comp," for short—is put together by an "organizer." The organizer hires a hotel with a dance space and blocks of rooms for dancers who are coming from far away, coordinates meals and prizes, and advertises the event throughout the dance world and by word of mouth. They hire a music master, entice vendors, publish a dance catalogue that lists all the heats and various prizes offered, and get tickets made up for the matinee and evening sessions. They offer prize money to lure top professionals to come and compete.

There are hundreds of comps during the year, of varying size and quality. Event organizers try to give each comp a nuance and exclusivity, frequently by setting decorative themes (like Mardi Gras or Halloween) or reflecting local culture. Comps usually run three days, but some are as short as one day, while some go up to five in order to accommodate a wider range of categories and age and skill levels.

There is no reason in the world a ballroom dancer needs to compete, ever. Ballroom dancing is a social sport, one that offers limitless grounds for refinement and self-development, much like playing a musical instrument purely for fun. It is an endlessly useful skill to develop, and there are plenty of opportunities to dance in any given community without ever leaving your comfort zone or friends, never mind being judged by a panel of strangers.

Competition isn't for everyone, either. For example, I thought it wasn't for me. I told Angelo as much the first day I met him. "There will be no competitions," I said. He nodded peaceably and cleverly didn't mention competitions again for three months, when he knew me and my psychology very well and knew exactly how best to weasel his way in.

Angelo is a very accomplished persuader—I still think he would have had a successful career as a salesman if dancing hadn't worked out for him. He casually mentioned a tiny local competition one day during my lesson, dropping it into conversation slyly. "Coincidentally, there happens to be a competition less than an hour from here in a couple of weeks," he said. "I thought maybe we could go and check it out, so you can see what other dancers are doing and what you'll look like as you keep improving." With his sales pitch, it didn't really occur to me that by agreeing to go I'd be competing against other dancers. He promised me the comp would be fun, that I should give it a try and see how I liked it, that is was very low commitment because it was so close and so small, and only one day. His clinching argument: it would be another opportunity to dance more, and wasn't dancing what I loved to do?

One of my Smooth dresses: notice all the tiny, intricate details—all ballroom dresses are made entirely by hand!

Despite Angelo's flawless pitch, I only told him I would think about it. It was my husband who eventually convinced me the comp was something I should try. He knew intuitively that I was resisting getting too involved in a hobby that was all about me (my husband is a beautiful social dancer, and we have lots of fun on the floor together, but he is not formally or competitively trained). Even though he wasn't dancing with me, he wanted me to know that he was behind me every step of my journey of discovery. In fact, he was pretty much shoving me down that path of discovery—he insisted I give the comp a chance, just to see if Angelo was right and I did really enjoy myself.

I realize, in retrospect, that Angelo and my husband have been totally in cahoots on my dance career since the very beginning. I suppose I owe those duplicitous men a thank-you, though, since it turned out they were right—I did end up enjoying competing, and it has pushed me to become a much better dancer.

Angelo wanted me to compete for my own development, of course, but dance teachers also make money from comps, since they are being paid for their time with you. Thus it is in their interest to persuade their students to do it. "Students are your business card," a teacher explained to me. As a teacher at a comp with your terrific student, you get noticed by everyone and your position in the dance world is enhanced.

Unfortunately, just learning the dance steps wasn't enough to prepare me for a comp. Once I agreed to give it a try, I had to go shopping.

The task of going to look at dance costumes was a terrible chore for me. Some people like to shop, I know, and for many women, trying on the fairytale ballroom dresses is probably one of their favorite parts of competing. Not for me, though. I don't enjoy trying things on, I hate crowds. I had promised Angelo I would think about getting a dress in case I wanted to compete, and unfortunately I couldn't just order one off the internet. I needed to have a costume that fit perfectly, which meant I had to go in and see the dresses in person.

I'm not the type of person who wants to drive 45 minutes to the mall. Going to look at my first ballroom dress was the first time in my life I had driven that far for any kind of shopping. Angelo accompanied me to a dress shop he knew to help me pick out all the things I would need—regulation shoes and dresses for each of the categories I would be dancing. I wouldn't let him drive me to the shop, because I still didn't know what kind of driver he would be. (He turned out to be perfectly safe in the end!)

There are very specific dress codes for any competition. For International Standard and American Smooth competitions, ladies must wear ball dresses with a hem length slightly above the ankle. All shoes must have a closed toe and a 2½ inch heel. I needed a long, sweeping ball dress—that is, a dress I could move in freely—and, since every tiny aspect of your personal presentation is factored into the judging, some earrings to match. I also had to buy flesh-colored satin pumps, like all female dancers. Although the heel is difficult to dance in, we all wear the highest heels we can under the regulations, since a higher heel contributes to a graceful leg line. With International Latin and American Rhythm competitions, ladies have a little more freedom in dress—your heel can be up to three inches high, and Latin costumes can be pretty exciting (I'm sure you have seen examples of a Latin costume in a movie or on TV).

As is the case in most dress-up scenarios, the gentlemen's costumes aren't quite as much fun as the ladies'. For International Standard and American Smooth, a dress suit or tails are required, as are patent leather

During a break, I try on a dress made by Deirdre Baker one of the
top ballroom dress makers. I am daring to show some skin on my back!

shoes. However, in the Latin and Rhythm divisions, the gents finally get to have a little fun, with an option of a plain or a ruffled shirt and shoes with the required Cuban heel, which is a slight high heel.

All ballroom dancing attire is carefully designed by former dancers. The dresses are painstakingly constructed—with bathing suits on the inside—to enable and embellish movement. It is also crucial that they are noticeable. All costumes are geared toward getting the judges' attention. The sparkle of the rhinestones and the bright colors are intended to create drama.

Every dress is made by hand, which is why they are so expensive. Some are made on spec. Many dancers rent dresses, since not everyone can afford to buy. Renting is a great way for beginners to see if this crazy scene is really for them—you don't even need to commit to a costume until you're ready.

I hated picking out the costumes. I hated the idea of it. It was commitment phobia, I realize now—in my heart I knew if I was spending money on a dress, I really did have to make good on my promise to Angelo to give this a shot. As well, I also disliked having to try on three different sets of required shoes (a closed pump for Standard, a sandal-type pump for Smooth, and yet another high-heeled sandal for Rhythm and Latin). They were, to me, intimidating.

Most of all, I hated how glamorous everything was. I felt ugly and old, and somehow unqualified to be playing a part in this dream scenario. I was frightened by them, and felt presumptuous to be trying on those beautiful works of art. The dresses were *real*, like an Olympic athlete's speed skating outfit or an NFL player's helmet. I felt that all those exquisite dresses and gewgaws didn't belong to a little nobody like me. They all looked beyond my reach. I didn't want to have to live up to my costume.

Ballroom dresses are often revealing, and I was shy about having so much of my skin exposed in front of my teacher. I was fifty-four years old, and standing there in the dress shop with the fluorescent lights glaring off the mirrors, I felt like a wrinkly old lady, ugly and curveless and ridiculous. My stomach twisted at the thought of Angelo, my trusted teacher and friend, with whom I had spent close and personal time every day for the last three months, seeing me in any of those flimsy, slippery creations. Angelo would be only the first of hundreds, possibly thousands, of people to see me in the costume, too. Not least among the strangers who would be staring at me in these were my future judges, who would be dissecting me with their eyes, looking for any sign of the sloppy, of the unpolished.

The shopkeeper and salesman who attended us, however, were very understanding and good-humored. They asked me if this would be my first competition, and they joked and put me at ease. Since then, I've realized this is the nature of most dance world vendors. They know about our inevitable nerves and are old pros at making this step, at least, a little bit easier.

I steered the shop owner toward dresses that covered as much of my skin as possible. I wanted to be wrapped up like a nun! Alas, a dancer needs considerable access to her limbs, and Angelo and the very helpful shop owner reminded me that the costumes I was seeing as exposing and embarrassing were actually designed to allow complete freedom of movement, thus letting the flow of my motions come through. The judges, after all, didn't care a fig how old I was or whether or not I had wrinkles. That had nothing to do with their points system at all.

In the end, I finally found shoes that fit my ice-skate blade thin feet. I rented the required long dress for American Smooth—mine was red, with long sleeves and a full skirt. I looked like an old-fashioned innocent. That was a style I felt comfortable with.

I bought, on sale, the requisite short dress for American Rhythm. It was a black and white Las Vegas showgirl-type dress, with fringe and see-through mesh over the back. I wasn't happy about having to wear such a short dress, but at least it didn't expose any bare skin except my legs, which would be covered with opaque stockings.

I had my costumes. This meant, of course, that I was committed. I was going to a comp. This was the beginning of my new reality.

his is the Developé, one of my favorite steps to do.
lets me show off my full skirt.

Chapter 4

First Time Showtime

*M*y husband and I left our house at 6 in the morning the day of my first competition, a small, one-day affair only a half an hour's drive from home. The car was full of "equipment"—dresses, shoes, hair bows, pills, pain killers, Gatorade, and a bag of tiny Tootsie Rolls.

I was in a foul mood. I was grumpy and irritable and couldn't remember why I'd agreed to do this. I sat in the car thinking about how much I stunk as a dancer. I resented the people who would be dancing on the floor next to me, competing against me.

Even at that miserable time, I recognized that it was my anxiety I was letting take over my mind. So I quieted myself down. I wasn't going to be a quitter. I had paid my participation money; I had made a commitment.

To be honest, I was terrified. I had made a deal with my husband: he would carry me onto the floor if I froze. I had no thoughts about winning—the idea that I could win at all had never even crossed my mind. I just wanted to remember the darn steps I had spent so many weeks practicing. I was, essentially, competing against myself.

Angelo and I would be what is called a pro-am couple, since he's a professional and I am an amateur. We'd only be competing against other pro-am couples.

As small and local as Angelo had promised this affair would be, the dressing room was anything but peaceful. I arrived just after 6:30 in the morning, and thank goodness I was there that early. The make-up areas were already starting to fill up, and, as I would see, they would be packed within the next hour.

Cranky with nerves, I changed into my dress and pinned up my hair into an arrangement that (after much practice) I knew would survive our most energetic spins. I've never been into dramatic makeup, but I did the best I could to play up my features so the judges would be able to see them from the floor. I was so nervous that my memories of that first morning and the two hours I spent getting ready are a haze of colors, sequins, tissues, and hairspray.

The dance catalogue had a schedule for the day, and Angelo collected our heat sheet, which listed all our dances and the approximate times those heats would be held. I'd be dancing in twenty-seven heats over the next five hours. I had to be on the floor for my first heat that day at 10 AM. Angelo, like all the male partners, was given four safety pins and a piece of paper with a number on it to wear on his back. He would keep that number all day; it was our couple number for the comp.

The floor was brightly lit by naked glaring bulbs, and looking out at the floor, I could only imagine how difficult it would be to keep my frame and to blink under that kind of spotlight. The temperature of the ballroom was meatlocker cold. I noticed the other female dancers around me were wearing dance jackets, leg warmers, coats, hoods, sometimes even mittens or gloves. As we waited for the heats to be called, some would get up to jump up and down or do jumping jacks. I would find out that this frigid "ballroom weather" was something all comps had in common, so the dancers working so aerobically on the floor wouldn't expire during the heats.

Waiting to take my turn on the flo
I am totally in the zone here
I don't remember having a thoug
in my head except the dance ste
Notice I'm wearing my dance jac
because the ballroom is so co

I didn't hear the Emcee announce my first heat, but Angelo and his wife did. Angelo took my hand—not just to steady my nerves; it's actually a requirement that a lady be lead onto the floor, and never go ahead of or without her teacher or partner—and guided me to our spot. I did make it onto the floor, stiff as a board but still vertical. Angelo nudged my arms into my dance position (which we call a "frame"). I was like a robot. Good for me.

Angelo is a giant—tall, muscular—and generally consumes a great deal of space. In this way, we are almost a comical team—I am narrow in just about every respect. When he positioned us on the floor, Angelo had to be careful that my back was to the judges. Otherwise, I would be completely obscured by his body and would never catch their eye.

I wish I could remember more about my first competitive heat, but I was nothing but nerves. I do remember the last thing Angelo said to me before the music started. He reminded me to keep my dance mask on at all times. Your dance mask is your still, placid smile (which I had not mastered yet). All dancers wear their dance mask every moment they are on the floor—the judges absolutely must not be able to tell how anxious or winded anyone is. The rule: breathe through your smile.

It was showtime—everything was in line and ready to go. was 100% concentrated on trying to remember my steps. I stared straight ahead at Angelo's face, probably looking like a deer in headlights, but I was too frightened to look at the whirling colors around me and too nearsighted to see anyone, anyway.

Still shocked by the feeling of having completed my first heat, I let Angelo lead me off the floor. I didn't realize I was still wearing my dance mask until I saw all the other dancers let their faces literally fall the

A Smooth dance.
During my first comp,
I was too nervous
to remember to smile.

Angelo towels off between heats.

moment they stepped off the polished wood. Moments earlier, they had been perfectly composed and dignified; now they were huffing and puffing, sucking out of water bottles, sloughing sweat off their foreheads, faces, necks.

Angelo sweats a lot. I had an inkling already, of course, since we had practiced together so many times. But it was only at my first comp that I learned exactly how much Angelo is capable of sweating.

The idea of dancing all those heats that first day sounded crazy to me, but there was a reason Angelo signed us up for as many as he did. You see, it's a matter of simple mathematics—the more heats you dance, the more points you'll have in the final tally.

Also, the more you are on the floor, the more familiar you become to the judging panel. This is both good and bad. It is good in that the judges will recognize you immediately as the day wears on, but it's bad in that the more familiar you are to them, the harder you have to work not to bore them. Every heat you dance has to be like a burst of light. Like any good entertainer, you have to try to become a light bulb that only goes out when you get off the stage floor.

Somehow, I made it through a bunch of heats that morning. They happened so quickly—that I didn't even have time to think about my nerves.

After my morning heats, I went to the dressing room to freshen up. There, I saw a woman I recognized—a fellow dancer whom I had met a few days before at a dress shop. We had chatted there and she had been really friendly to me. I had seen her on the floor that morning, as well—in fact, I'd beaten her in a couple of heats. When I saw her now in the dressing room, I gave her a big wave and a loud, "Hi!"

My heart plummeted at her reaction. She barely lifted her lips into a sneer and turned away. I couldn't believe it. I had to fight down my anger because I knew that getting mad at another competitor wasn't in the gracious spirit of ballroom dancing. I would, however, get even. I was going to beat the pants off her. In retrospect, I owe a lot to that woman. She was the one who showed me how competitive I could be!

After a short break for lunch, the afternoon whizzed by in another storm of heats and colors. When the voice came over the speaker to announce the competition was over, I found, to my surprise, that I felt elated. Angelo had been right—competing wasn't horrible at all. It just triggered in me a huge sense of accomplishment and triumph. After three months of ballroom dancing in the studio, I wasn't just dancing by and for myself anymore. I was a part of something a little bit larger, a community of like-minded artists.

What I was not expecting to hear was my own name among the award winners. I had somehow won Top Student in the competition! I was so shocked that I was almost delirious with gratitude—to the judges, my teacher, my husband, the whole world! I was so blessed to have found something I loved that, apparently, I was also good at.

Many competitions have participation awards, and I have collected a number of them. But this one, my first ever, will always be special to me.

I gratefully receive an award at a comp in Miami.

Chapter 5

GETTING INTO THE COMPETITION SWING

I was headed down the path toward a dancing addiction anyway, but my first competition (and first victory) pushed me over the edge. Since that fateful day, my life had become dancing. Angelo and I were practicing three hours a day, five days a week.

When I wasn't practicing with Angelo, my schedule included the following (and just about nothing else): stretching, eating, stretching again, sleeping, swimming, stretching, and—somewhere in there—my job. I have to admit that my brain became a little monothematic during that period. I would sit at my desk paging through my emails, but all to the tune of Waltz music in my head, my feet moving under my chair in miniature box steps. I started waking myself up by accident because I was doing dance steps in my sleep. I would catch myself singing all the time. I was happy.

THE WALTZ

The Waltz, perhaps the most famously familiar and yet notoriously difficult of all dances, is the music of the spheres. Its feeling is all curves and arches and circles. The Waltz has an ancient and accessible beat: *ONE, two, three*. One could almost say that is the quintessential dance beat. The Waltz is an old dance with peasant roots, and for this reason it feels like it has been an art form in its current five-step formation for almost three hundred years.

From Austria, it rose to popularity in Europe in the late 18th century and quickly became the template for many other developing types of ballroom dances. The Waltz is such a wonderful framework for movement and emotion that many forms and genres of Waltzes have developed over the centuries.

The competitive ballroom Waltzes, however, are very specific dances. The International Standard Waltz is a hallmark dance of chivalry and propriety, a measured and yet intimate dance where the partners are close to each other throughout, meaning we almost never separate or leave our dance frame. The American Smooth Waltz, on the other hand, has lots of separations and flourishes.

The trick to Waltzing well is to control the music, not to let the music control you. Making the transition from beat to beat is challenging—your movements should be very fluid, with nary a hiccup. I still hiccup. I adore the Waltz. The music is always melodic and the most romantic of all the dances. It is a giddy, dreamy dance.

The Basic Box Turn, and then onto Twinkles in the American Waltz.

As the intensity of my practicing built up, Angelo added new dance categories to our repertoire. This is when he started teaching me the International dances, and, to help me cement them in my knowledge quickly, he convinced me to sign up for a second competition only three months after my first victory.

I was competing against other Bronze-level amateurs like me. The levels are more stratified than simply who has more experience—they also dictate the steps a dancer performs in a given dance. All competitors, amateurs and professionals alike, are judged on how well they execute their steps. However, every single step we take in each dance is regulated and judged by very specific rules; we must work within the very prescribed framework.

There are a lot of rules for Bronze-level dancers. We are allowed no syncopated timing or double spins. Unlike Silver and Gold dancers, we are judged by how clearly we perform the basic steps. As we get better and as our technique evolves, we graduate to Silver- and then Gold-level rules, where the steps are more and more complicated.

Occasionally, the master of ceremonies will remind competitors to please be sure they are dancing "in category" and that they will be penalized if they use steps or choreography that is not appropriate to their level. This, of course, is the teacher's responsibility.

For me and my fellow Bronze-level competitors, our challenge is to perfect our syllabus, to demonstrate that we are competent and qualified in the dances at their most straightforward, and—if we can—to learn to express ourselves within the close confines of the rules. Excellent Bronze-level dancing is like a well-played Bach fugue. All students are doing the identical mix of steps. Those who stand out and grab the atten-

We do the Hustle, a dance I love, with an Inside Spin into a

tion of the judges are the ones who manage this most basic task with grace, poise, and energy.

This way, we perfect our basic knowledge—feet first, then add arms. Meanwhile, we develop the ability to express ourselves—in a situation where, it seems, we have no freedom at all. If we can learn to put some personality into the steps in this most rigid framework, imagine the potential we develop to express ourselves as we progress.

Within each of these levels, Bronze, Silver, and Gold, there are further breakdowns so you can compete more fairly with those at your level. For Bronze, I began as Newcomer, a level I could only dance for one year throughout the circuit. Then, I moved up to Beginner (or Novice), then Intermediate, then Full. Sometimes, comp names for each of these divisions will vary, but the breakdown is always the same.

Finally, because a 35-year-old will usually (but not always) dance with more agility than a 75-year-old, there is an age category breakdown, too.

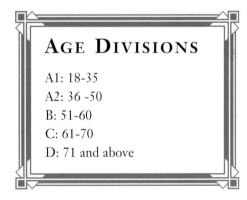

AGE DIVISIONS

A1: 18-35
A2: 36 -50
B: 51-60
C: 61-70
D: 71 and above

There are Youth and Junior divisions, as well. Dancers are allowed to dance in their age category and the one just below theirs, but they are not allowed to dance the level above.

Maybe it was all the new dances I was going to be competing in, but I wasn't much less nervous at my second comp than I had been at my first. It was a larger comp this time, a three-day affair in Miami Beach. I was competing against a lot more people than I had the first time. I think this is when I began to realize that I was never going to feel "ready" before a competition. The second comp was a bit bewildering as I was still in my robot mode. It felt a bit like being a soldier, or like a horse that has been blinkered just to stay in its track. I was in step-memorization mode, only looking at Angelo's face to confirm my steps, with my ear constantly alert to the music. I tuned out any other stimuli. In the end, it worked.

Angelo did his best to calm me down. He repeatedly expressed his unflagging confidence in me. "Relax, Lydia," he said, I don't know how many times. "You're going to place well. Just watch." He was right—I won Top Student again! I felt like daisies were falling from the sky! I was so exhilarated. Every breath was like inhaling stardust. It was an intoxicating emotion.

Looking at the pictures of my second competition, I can see my nerves. I hadn't learned yet that I shouldn't splay the fingers of my left hand all over Angelo's shoulder like a bunch of bananas. I also hadn't yet learned to smile. It would take me a couple more competitions to make that very important breakthrough.

By the New Orleans comp, I'm star
learn to

SWING

Swing is one of the most easygoing and fun of the dances, which is one of the reasons it has become such a popular social dance all over America, even outside of the ballroom world. There is enormous variety in the steps, and something about the dance feels wholly American.

"Swing" describes a number of kinds of dances, but they all find their roots in the mid-20th century American jazz and Big Band traditions. The inspiration for the modern Swing goes back to the Lindy Hop during Prohibition and traces its way through the Jitterbug, the Blues, the Jive, and Rock and Roll. As such, Swing became one of the earliest competitive dances, with bona fide large-scale dance-offs popping up in ballrooms across America and abroad in the late 1920s. Like many of the greatest and most American cultural hallmarks, Swing dancing originated in the black community in the early 1920s, when it was paired with the newly popular jazz music.

Part of the reason I couldn't entirely shake my nerves was the fact that you never know exactly what is going to happen at a comp. No matter how much you've practiced your steps, there are external factors all around you that can throw a wrench into your smooth routine.

Despite the precise order of dances laid out in the catalogue at each comp, there are always unforeseen circumstances that occasionally result in the heat order being switched, and it is not uncommon for heats to run ahead or behind the printed schedule. As a result, it is imperative that dancers be in the ballroom at least half an hour before their heat's scheduled time (and at larger comps, you have to be in the ballroom forty-five minutes early). Emcees generally go to extra lengths to make sure all dancers are present for heats.

Dancers are supposed to be in the on-deck area, near the dais, at least one dance before they go on. The heat number is called, and the teachers rush to find the space they want on the floor. The Emcee announces the category, dance level, and age group, sometimes calling out the numbers of the competitors on the floor. Then he signals the beginning of the heat by calling, "Music, please!" Depending on how many competitors there are in a heat, there may be quarter-finals, semi-finals, and finals, with a number of couples eliminated at each stage.

All pros have a theater persona and most have a sense of carnival, or a delicious bit of vaudeville. They also have an innate sense of humor, often slapstick—Punch and Judy, and Three Stooges-esque—that is timeless, innocent, and hilarious. Every pro and teacher I've ever met is a quintessential show person. They love to be center stage, know how to play and flirt with the audience—any audience, including one another—and love to have a good time. They have to retain their humor, since their career requires them to teach people a new skill, to make students feel comfortable, and to help everyone laugh off their mistakes.

Very funny things can happen in a ballroom, which can relieve the tension for everyone and pick up the mood. This happens particularly in the mid-afternoon, when we've all been on the floor for hours and our energy starts to lag. The teachers and pros, consummate entertainers, go to efforts to make sure the judges aren't getting bored with unenergetic dancing. They pump it up. Some strategies include intentional bodily contact with other couples, before, during, or after the heats—usually a little bump on the derrière—or a ridiculous comment (within earshot) about another teacher's appearance or dancing abilities. Some teachers will call out kiss-up comments to judges right in the middle of a heat—all in good humor and fun.

Angelo fools around during a heat.

Other times, one teacher will snatch another teacher's student as the couples are walking out onto the dance floor, much to the amusement and bewilderment of the student. This is always a fun adventure, since it is all done in the spirit of mixing it up. You always think, *Am I really going to dance with another teacher?!* The answer is always no.

Off the floor and in between heats, there are no end of ad lib comedic performances. I have seen napkins, face towels, and cups become magic tricks, talking hand puppets, and medieval weapons. One teacher, famous for his *bon vivant* approach to comps—so much so that he often wins Top Teacher—makes flatulent noises, swears, or stops to have sips of coffee during a heat, leaving his student on the floor. Like other teachers, he will occasionally dance right off the floor and onto the carpet. Slapstick is a way of life among teachers, and there is always a great deal of falling down, dropping dead, tripping, and pretending to vomit. It is like playing with a bunch of overgrown kids and is a wonderful way to diffuse the tension.

On occasion, the music master himself will sense that a dullness has settled over the ballroom, or that the level of tension has gotten too high, so at a costume break or a heat change, "YMCA" comes on! If an outsider happened upon the ballroom at this point, he would find the entire population of dancers, ticket takers, photographers, audience—even the judges!—in a state of collective disco fever. Pencils and papers drop to the floor, everyone stops whatever they are doing, and the entire competition waves their arms in the YMCA dance, with everyone singing along to the words. I wish this happened more often.

Make no mistake—while we do have fun moments, a comp is serious business. There are reputations to uphold and new ones to make. There are champions starting out and older ones clinging to fading glory; there are dreams hatching and dreams going up in smoke; and, lest we forget, this is a for-profit enterprise. A good comp can be very profitable for its organizers, prize money can be sizable for teachers and professional champions, and there are a lot of jobs being fulfilled, from teachers to musicians to judges to floor sweepers. This is a business where commerce and art come together in a magnificent partnership.

My third comp was the prestigious Ohio Star Ball, which ran for five days, from November 16th through 21st. The Ohio Star Ball is the Olympics of competitive ballroom dancing. It is the official end of one dance calendar year for the DanceSport Series and the beginning of the next, where all the points accumulated by dancers are tallied for this year's prizes, then erased, so everyone begins with a clean slate. Coming to Ohio is a very big deal.

I have to admit that Ohio felt like the real beginning of my competitive dancing career. The first two comps were lucky timing, a boost for my confidence, but I hadn't really locked into the community. With Ohio, I felt like I was having an official debut.

Angelo and I arrived early and, wearing practice clothes, ran through some routines on the enormous dance floor. Most teachers and pupils do this. The hope is to get a feel for the floor and to get in the zone before the extraneous stresses of the competition begin.

The Ohio ballroom has two huge dance floors and houses the dreams of thousands of competitors from all over the world. Literally thousands of dancers in all age ranges—from 3 to 90—and divisions take part in the six days of competition. It is here that the amateurs, pro-ams, and professionals will compete for a title of US Champion in a multitude of categories, and where the Top Student and other prizes are awarded. The couples who win will hold their title for the subsequent year. This gives them prestige, credibility, and endorsements, which lead studios

and comp organizers to hire them to do shows. Ohio is the Land of Oz, the pot of gold at the end of the rainbow.

The intrepid and good-humored organizer, Sam Sodano, is a former champion himself. He is the founder of the Ohio Star Ball. He is the "godfather," as he says, of modern ballroom dance. When I complimented him on the video recordings I had seen of his dancing, he said, "What do you mean I was great? I was perfect!"

Sam looks like a Roman senator of yore, with astonishing clear green eyes. He also has a dramatic presence and an enormous amount of charisma. He has fought for the better part of twenty years to keep ballroom dancing alive in the United States, from the time when ballroom popularity was at its recent lowest through its current golden age. For many of the last fifteen years, he has managed to get the professional competitions at the Ohio Star Ball televised on PBS to make the competition available to enthusiasts across the country.

Sam also started the DanceSport Series for pro-ams like myself. This is the dance category where there competitors are not restricted to their division steps, so even Bronze dancers like me can dance Gold steps or above. I love this bracket of competition, because it allows the showy moves that I wouldn't be allowed to dance for years otherwise—drops, splits, anything within the framework of the one rule, which is that one foot must remain on the floor. (That's the rule of which you always see the judges on "Dancing with the Stars" reminding the contestants!)

Angelo signed me up for this category during my first year of dancing, which was ridiculous, since I was the only Bronze dancer competing against Silver and full Gold dancers. But it was also by far the most fun of all my dances, and what I looked forward to the most during my comps. I could dance the complete phrases of music in American Smooth Open and Rhythm without having to close my feet like I have to in Bronze. I could do three spins in a row, and show off my drops and splits. I had no illusions that I would win in any of these categories, but I loved to dance them because they were pure bliss.

This is the brilliance of Sam. He has inspired people to push their level of dance much higher than they thought they would ever be able by competing against other couples of all levels in closed and open categories.

During the Ohio Star Ball, participants occupy every nook and cranny of all the rooms in three very large hotels in downtown Columbus. For the full six days and nights, dancers flood the restaurants, escalators, elevators, stairs, bathrooms, and walkways of the complex. There are more sequins and more tension at this comp than at any other. The practice rooms are packed to the gills. It is a 24/7 competition, the toughest comp in the country, with the largest number of competitors, all of whom have come to *win*. This is no comp for social dancing; it is hard core competition. The Ohio Star Ball is not for the faint of heart.

I would be lying if I said I wasn't terrified. The idea of the Ohio Star Ball was overwhelming at first, but then I got over it. So what, I told myself. No one's life was at stake. At fifty-four years old, did I care more about my pride or my desire to dance? That's how much, I had realized, I loved to dance—my passion overrode even my shrinking violet instincts. I just wanted to dance and feel the adrenalin. That's all.

It always helped me to remember that I was the lowest critter on the totem pole at these comps, at the absolute bottom of the hierar-

One of the two huge ballroo
at the Ohio Star B.

chy in the dance world, and I loved it! There was nowhere to move but up.

I had no expectations of winning anything at the Ohio Star Ball. I was delighted to discover that we actually made a few call-backs, but that wasn't what really mattered to me. What awed me was the discovery that there were so many other women who were doing what I was. This world was huge! I liked the space and scope it offered. I loved the adrenaline of dancing with so many other couples on the floor. I thought all my competitors were beautiful. They were all talented. They were all dancers! This was the big world of ballroom dance! Angelo had told me that if this comp didn't put me off, none of them would. It didn't. It made me want to do as many comps as I could. Bring it on!

There were, however, plenty of other dancers at the Ohio Star Ball who weren't having as grand a time of it as I was. There were newcomers throwing up in the bathrooms, sobbing in the dressing rooms, or having hysterics in the corners. There were some dancers whose plumbing went haywire from nerves and who were dashing off to the lavatories every two minutes; others got faint from anxiety and had to be shepherded over to resting places by their teachers. There were some dancers who hyperventilated or got dry mouth or the shakes. There were some who just left. I was luckier; I just went into robot mode. I was an unsmiling robot, but at least an erect and functioning robot.

I have seen women sobbing uncontrollably after losing a serious dance comp. Sometimes these weeping women are students, sometimes they are professionals. It is awful to see because you know that they have tried their best, but something didn't go right. Not everyone always gets a second chance. This is the nature of competition.

We are in the on-deck area with other couples, waiting to take the floor for our next heat. I was awed by the number of other dancers at the Ohio Star Ball. Being there made me excited to realize there was a thriving community of people who loved to dance as much as I did.

To get us used to the dance floor before the competition starts, Angelo always takes me out and we run through routines in our warm up clothes. Being on the huge Ohio floor by ourselves was a little surreal.

Now, old hat that I am, I have a routine for brainwashing myself before I have to go out on the floor. Each time I wait for my heat to be called, I repeat to myself, "I am a dancer, I am a dancer, I am a dancer." If I am feeling wimpy or hesitant, I call up the image of a particular photograph of my grandfather. In it, he looks out from the bridge of his ship, the *USS Augusta*, on the critical gray morning of D-Day in World War II, as the Admiral in charge of the invading American naval forces. To me, his face looks like one of the determined and confident visages on Mt. Rushmore. I remind myself that if he could cross the English Channel with the responsibility of that many lives in his hands, I can darn well get out there on the floor and dance.

gelo and I compete at first Ohio Star Ball.

Chapter 6
ON THE ROAD

"*I*'ll widen your world," Angelo told me.

"Really?" I quipped.

"Yes, really," he said. He wasn't kidding.

In the airport in Charlotteville, North Carolina, I entered my first sports bar—not entirely of my own free will. It was actually of Angelo's free will. I ordered a bottle of water and dialed my sister, Deborah, to tell her where I was. She could not stop laughing—*A sports bar, Lydia? I thought I'd never see the day!*

That was the inauguration of our Sports Bar Tour of America. As it turns out, airports and hotels all over the United States have sports bars with multiple giant flat screen TVs and people of all ages eating ribs, hamburgers, tacos, shrimp buckets, and club sandwiches, all of which are, apparently, served with about a pound of French fries. Happily for me— I don't eat fried foods or drink alcohol—sports bars almost always have a Caesar salad on their menu. No fries come with that.

Despite certain consistencies in dinner menus across the country— I'm still mystified by the universal application of cheese to just about everything—sports bars are always interesting, according to Angelo, because of the variety of beers on the menu. He is a moderate drinker who prefers quality over quantity, and nothing is quite as exciting as a new regional premium beer. Often, the beers served change from region to region. Over our years of extensive research, the largest selection we have come across to date was in Milwaukee. Angelo was popeyed.

I also learned from my adventures with Angelo that there is a particular sports patois spoken all over the United States. Sports bar atmosphere, it turns out, is always friendly, casual, and tolerant of the whoops and shouts for any particular team. One place you *cannot* talk about a rival team is in Ohio, home of the Buckeyes. If you happen to mention Michigan in Ohio—which Angelo, who likes to stir up the pot, decided to give a go—you will be lucky if you escape without a brawl.

Angelo also introduced me to the world of fast food. I had never had any before, believe it or not, except McDonalds, a restaurant I'd been to back in the 1970s. I had eaten a McBurger maybe seven times in my life. Angelo, however, is a big fan of cheeseburgers. He has not converted me, but he has turned me onto Subway, my favorite fast food place. Their chicken soup and a turkey swiss wrap with lettuce, oil, vinegar, and extra tomatoes really hits the spot.

Whenever we're headed to a local comp—any comp in Region 3, my U.S. dance region, which includes Florida—we drive. We stock up on food for the trip and the comp: water, Gatorade, snacks, Tootsie Rolls, and chocolate bars for Angelo. We both take our iPods, but in the car we sing along to Angelo's comprehensive Eagles collection. Our singing abilities are less refined than our dancing, but sing we do, and at the top of our lungs. Angelo adds some percussion by honking the horn if he is very moved, or braking to the rhythm if we are stuck in traffic. His truck is extremely sound proof, so we can wail our way down four hours of highway without disturbing other drivers.

With the Ohio Star Ball behind us, I found I liked comps. Ohio had been a grind—overwhelming, intensely exciting, dramatic, fierce. Ohio had given me a deep look into the anatomy of the ballroom dance world at its highest level, for amateurs and for pros. I had seen what the possibilities were for a dancer like me, and I was eager to push on.

We were now doing up to 160 heats at each comp. With the Opens and Scholarships, and the possibility of call-backs as dancers are eliminated in big heats, the comps we attended became filled with dancing! Of course I was not on the floor continually; we would go on for six heats, off for six, on for twelve, off for twenty, and so it would flow throughout the day. What this meant as well was that there could be a lot of waiting time between heats, giving me a chance to run to the ladies' room, have a drink of water, or eat a food bar. I still had to stay focused, and be sure I put my warm-up jacket on. As the day rolled on, other levels would start to do their heats, giving us time for lunch or a costume change. Always, though, we had to watch the progression of the comp carefully so we were in the on-deck area on time for our next heat, pumped and ready to dance.

Over January, February, and March, Angelo and I attended a whirlwind of comps: Dance Heat in Delray, Florida; The Winter Ball in Greenbrier, West Virginia; The Heritage Classic in Ashville, North Carolina; and The Southern States in New Orleans. Sometime around New Orleans, I realized that I had become confident enough that I was making it out onto the floor with a smile on my face.

At the New Orleans comp. All the couples are doing Crossovers in the Cha-Cha.

Not only was I gaining confidence, but, to my utter bewilderment, I was winning. I wasn't just winning lots of my heats. I was consistently taking Top Bronze Student and even Top Student prizes. I seemed to be winning all the time, which felt weird. A good weird.

I was surprised every time I was awarded a prize, but at least, at this point, I was beginning to understand what the judges were judging me on. Your shape, size, and height don't matter. Judges look for precision, attitude, confidence, showmanship, fluidity, and tempo control. They also monitor a couple's frame—that is, how they hold each other—and their connection. There should be the right amount of pressure and control between two dancers, who should be well-balanced, with sharp, sure posture. Left hand fingers should be closed, not open. Heads and eyes should be pointing toward the ceiling. If dancers forget these niceties, the judges dock points.

Judges also watch your floor craft—that is, how you navigate around the dance floor as a team, following the dictated counter-clockwise Line of Dance (or LOD). They watch to make sure you and your partner are not bumping or smashing into other couples or breaking your own routine, and that you recover smoothly if you do.

The judging of a competition is a very complicated and carefully orchestrated affair. Every competition requires a board of adjudicators to evaluate the dancers. A non-championship competition requires a minimum of three Judges, but if the prize money is more than $1,000, there must be at least five Judges. In a championship competition, a minimum of seven Judges are required.

Besides Judges, there are a number of other dance professionals present at any competition, all of whom have passed rigorous exams set by either the National Dance Council of America (NDCA) or the

The joint is jumping to the Jive at the Dallas comp.

British Dance Council, etc. There are always at least two scrutineers, who collate the Judges' score sheets from each heat, tally the results, and generally officiate to make sure everything goes smoothly on the floor. A chairman is required to officiate at every NDCA competition, and if a competition has more than 4,000 entries or extends over 4 or more days two chairmen are required. There is also an observer at any NDCA competition. The observer verifies that all aspects of the comp are up to NDCA standards. This covers everything from making sure there are adequate restroom and changing facilities, sufficient dance floor size, suitable lighting, and appropriate safety precautions. Finally, there is an invigilator, who makes sure that all dancers are using the correct steps appropriate to the level they are dancing. The invigilator is the one responsible for disqualifying those who do not adhere to the strict syllabus of steps for each level.

The organizer of each competition is responsible for inviting the appropriate number of judges, scrutineers, and administrators from the NDCA roster. The organizer is also responsible for making sure all the facilities are up to snuff. There are myriad other aspects of a competition that are easy to overlook as a competitor or audience member but of which the organizers keep very careful track.

For example, the organizer must coordinate all the heats. Each NDCA pro-am heat usually runs for one minute and twenty seconds, and there must be twenty seconds between heats. Solo dances must be timed for three minutes and Championship heats for two minutes. The music, of course, must correspond exactly, and the organizer must make sure that the music selection falls within the parameters of NDCA regulations.

Judges are always dancers or former dancers. Often, they are former champions. In order to become judges, they must pass a rigorous exam-

I am always so pleased to receive placement awards after a series of heats.

ination. This, of course, is on top of the practical experience they have over their years out on the floor, circling through the same time-honored competitions they are now judging.

Judging an art form is, of course, very subjective as well as objective. Each judge is qualified in all dances, and often a judge has a specialty, something specific they look for in a dancer or a team, something that comes closest to their particular ideas of perfect form. In any given heat, there are lots of swirling bodies, often moving very quickly to the music and spending mere seconds in front of the judges. It is mind-boggling to me that the judges are somehow expected to evaluate all the dancers in the short eighty seconds they have to watch the floor. In the end, they reward the couples who execute the steps well and who catch their attention most vibrantly.

Usually, there is a high correlation between the eye-catching couples and the talented couples—perfection of form and artistic flare certainly help the judges separate the winners from the crowd. The better a dancer is at the actual maneuvers, the harder it is to look away while they are dancing. Couples who work well together tend to look sharper and smoother, thereby drawing attention to themselves. Punctual phrasing—that is, dovetailing dance steps with the beats of the music—is another feat of talented dancers that helps attract the judges' notice. The more accurately a couple's choreography coordinates with the music they are dancing to, the more likely they will stand out from less perfectly phrased couples.

There are other factors that contribute to a dancer's ability to rise above the fray: judges get bored. They want to be entertained. The key aspect of becoming a good dancer is learning the art of entertainment. This is why we dancers pay such close attention to our appearance and

This is the sheet the judges use to score each dance and dancer. Based on the tallied results, judges will invite couples back to dance callbacks for quarter-finals, semi-finals, and finals in each dance.

It's important to let the judges notic you during a heat. Here, Angelo and I do a Overdrop Sway directly in front of the judges

try to make our hair and costumes as dazzling as possible. I still wonder if I didn't win my first comp at least in part because of the bright red dress I wore.

I know that I can't control the outcome of a competition at all. There are times when I know I have been the best dancer on the floor but I haven't won that comp, because for whatever reason I was overlooked. At the same time, I felt there have been times when I took home the first prize and I knew there were other dancers better than I was. Although some dancers get upset when they don't believe the outcome of a competition is what they deserved, I don't construe this as unfairness. Judges don't have instant replay to fall back on; they must make decisions based on quick impressions. For this reason, it's important to be your own most critical judge.

I have, however, been known to get upset at myself when I think I didn't dance well enough, even when the judges have awarded me a prize. *I know I let my frame down in that Quick Step*, I have thought to myself, or, *I wish I had remembered to change my weight in our last Whisk.* That kind of judgment—my own—makes me angry. I hate being any less than perfect.

In fact, I never—ever—feel ready for a comp. I am never going to be as refined in my movements as I want to be. I'll never have quite as much control over my body as I wish I had. In part, this is because I become more refined and more controlled everyday, and because everyday there are new levels of achievement I suddenly realize are possible for me. *Am I remembering to tuck my head right? Will my arm extensions be graceful enough? Will I get the correct hip movement in the Merengue?*

A week before each comp I would decide I didn't want to go. I would even find specific excuses why I couldn't possibly attend this one event—

In the American Foxtrot, we do a Release to Open Twinkle.

THE FOXTROT

The Foxtrot is a ragtime classic, with a distinctive *slow-slow-quick-quick* rhythm. The dance is named for vaudeville actor Harry Fox, who danced an early version of the famous stagger steps in 1914. It was the most popular fast dance during the whole first half of the twentieth century.

The Foxtrot is a ballroom phenomenon. For competitors, it is a complicated dance that allows for much flexibility and style with its slow, syncopated 4/4 rhythm. But there's also a social version of the Foxtrot that is perennially popular with beginners and in crowded dancehalls.

It is the most difficult of the Smooth dances. I find that the tempo of the Foxtrot is even more challenging to control than that of the Waltz. It is the most "pure" American form of ballroom dance, since it is so rooted in American musical and popular culture. Its character is bubbly, sassy, flirtatious—it's a Broadway Musical kind of dance. Fred and Ginger were masters of the Foxtrot. Angelo has a wonderful Foxtrot—I am still learning how to be bubbly!

Angelo and I execute a Basic, then a Back-to-Back, and return to a Basic in the American Foxtrot.

my back/ankle/neck/leg hurt; I didn't have the energy to pack; I hadn't had nearly enough time to practice the steps I would need to know well for this next leg of the journey. The destination city was freezing at this time of year—why would I want to subject myself to that when I could be at home on the beach?

This, of course, would be my nerves talking. I've found during competitions that a dancer's state of anxiety can be mapped nicely by a bell curve. When Angelo first talks me into going, everything seems fine. As the day approaches, my worries coalesce, and I begin to fret about all the pieces of my performance. There is no time I am less sure of the steps on a dance floor than those days before a comp, when I might be practicing my most sure-footed Foxtrot and suddenly find my mind is blank and I can't remember the next step.

My inner coach is very persuasive, though; in fact, somewhat to my surprise, she is quite formidable. More than anything she hates to give up. During my worst moments of fear and anxiety, my inner coach pushes her way to the front of my mind, reminds me of the promise I made to myself, and coaxes me through the steps. We work them together, my inner coach and I, perhaps a little obsessively, until they are smooth and I have remembered that I am a Dancer. She sets me clear goals for the immediate future and tells me I *must* achieve them, no excuses. I would *never* give up! It was do or die! I discussed my commitment quite seriously with my husband, and we agreed that if I did die on the dance floor, that would be just fine. Well, not fine, but preferable to letting anything stop me from getting to the dance floor. This was what I was going to do.

Sometimes, I have another mini-attack of nerves the morning of the competition itself. When the alarm clock goes off at five in the morning,

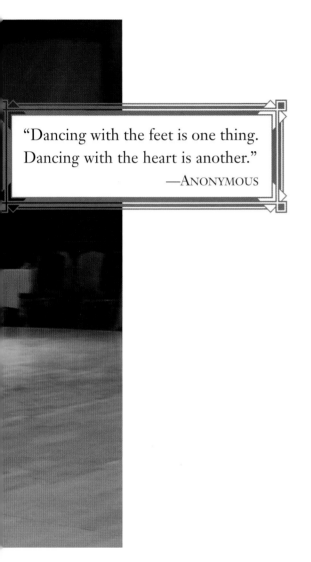

> "Dancing with the feet is one thing. Dancing with the heart is another."
>
> —ANONYMOUS

my eyes open to my shadowy hotel room, only the grayest crepuscular light sneaking its way through the blinds. I feel the ache in the balls of my feet, in my ankles, my back, and realize beyond any doubt that I can't get out of bed that morning, that my body has given up and I will never be able to make it pull itself erect, never mind dance. But then—with the help of that stubborn, pig-headed inner coach of mine—I do.

The truth is that we dance because we love to dance, and that truth is utterly unconnected with nerves. In my most nervous moments, I always ask myself, "What else would I rather be doing today?" My answer is always the same—"There is nothing I would rather be doing than dancing." When I get over that mental speed bump and recommit myself, the nerves lessen, and I can honestly tell you that the moment Angelo leads me onto the floor at the start of a heat, there is nothing in my mind but the steps, crystal concentration, the music, the energy flowing through my limbs.

The anxiety bell curve, a product of my own self-consciousness, is my toxic enemy, but it is also the enemy of every other dancer swirling across those gleaming floorboards with me. While the most experienced dancers may have very shallow anxiety bells, I can tell you with confidence that not many dancers would honestly be able to say they have no nerves before a competition at all. I try to harness this thought and hold onto it during my darkest moments. The truth is, we are all in the same boat—we all want to do our personal best, and we all have the same fears. Remembering this helps me see my competitors as family—I am not alone.

I used to hate airplanes, and all of my touring didn't change that. By my seventh comp in New Orleans, however, I was beginning to get used to the flying. In my opinion, there is no reason to get on an airplane unless you *really* want to get to your destination. I knew that in order to dance, I needed to get myself from point A to point B, and it helped me to remember the miraculous healing power of the adrenalin I would feel when I finally was dancing. Also, Angelo had to hold my hand during take-off and landing. But one of my recent great joys in life is that my plane-phobia has essentially been replaced with dance mania.

Often, my husband came along as our dance manager, taking photos, helping me get myself together in the morning, and generally being enthusiastic about my crazed venture. He was a source of energy and stability when he was there with me.

At the comps, we rarely had time for much sightseeing. The days are filled with early risings, frantic preparations, flurries of dance heats, and intense exhaustion. But even in the hotels, you get a flavor of the area of the United States you are visiting. America is a wonderfully diverse country with a full palate of regional cultures, and comp Organizers do everything they can to bring some of that flavor to the comp itself.

By the New Orleans comp, I was starting to get to know a number of other couples in my categories. Many of us were in the same situation, dancing in this competitive circle for the first time, and as a result I could feel our collective energies building each time our paths intersected at another comp. I didn't realize it at the time, but we were a growing family of dancers.

The competitions are filled with wonderful, gracious, hardworking dancers that I'm sure I would love to get to know better. At least, I think they are. To be honest, my mind is concentrated so intensely on the dance I am about to do that I rarely interact with other competitors or teachers. I try not to fall into the tempting trap of gossiping in the hair-

A Crossover in the Bolero

dressing rooms or accidentally eavesdropping on other people's conversations. In the end, other people's opinions of my dancing, should they come up, are only destabilizing to me. If I hear people criticizing my dancing, of course I feel bad about myself; if I hear them praising it, I begin to feel self-conscious and pressured to uphold their standards when really only dancing my best should matter.

Angelo, of course, also demands a large portion of my personal attention. He likes to keep me slightly apart from the crowds, for my own psychological wellbeing as well as to offer me constant coaching and advice. Angelo keeps me in dance mode, since the person I present off the dance floor is the person I am likely to be on the dance floor as well. I do my best to be graceful and gracious, smiling and poised, and to have good posture and deliberate movements all the time. In this way, dancers carry dancing around with them everywhere.

To further impersonalize my competition experience, I am nearsighted. I can't wear glasses on the ballroom dance floor—there is risk that they might fall or be knocked off—so I can't see anyone's face at all, particularly the judges'. The people dancing around me are swirls of color and black and white. Only Angelo is real, and that is because he is tangible, damp and muscular at the ends of my fingertips, always there to lead me onto the next step.

The second language of American ballroom dancing is Russian, although there are professionals and teachers from all over the world. There is a dynamic sense of fervor among recent immigrants, who have brought with them the intensity of training and discipline from their home countries, many of which have always treated ballroom dancing as a very serious sport and part of their cultural heritage. At the same time, there is a deep patriotism in the United States competitive circuits. No

Angelo and I execute a Featherstep in the International Foxtrot while a judge wrotes on his score sheet.

one ever talks politics, but at every comp there is an American flag on full display.

Once we finish dancing for the day, Angelo usually lets me sneak off to my room, where I collapse to stretch in front of the TV while I watch "Law & Order" and the Weather Channel. Even though ballroom dancing started as a social activity, the comps are anything but a social occasion for a student at my level.

Once all the students have done dancing for the day, they get a reward: the chance to see the professionals compete. If it's a large competition, we might also get to see a professional couple do a show, as well. This is the big time. This is when you get to see perfection.

Just as there are stars in the world of ballet and opera, there are also stars in the world of ballroom dance, and big general public audiences will travel for miles to come watch these brilliant dancers and cheer for their favorite couple. The crowds who arrive on the Friday or Saturday nights usually get dressed up, somtimes in evening clothes, because it is a formal and very dramatic event. The professionals compete for titles and for cash awards.

The beauty of the professional competitors' dancing is dazzling. Their power, precision, speed, is as astonishing to watch as that of an Olympic figure skater. To watch them is to know what human beings are capable of when they are at their best. It makes me happy to be alive to know that these dancers not only exist but are increasing in number everyday.

I have no pretense of ever achieving the brilliance of these professionals. I know I will never be close, not even within a mile, certainly not in my lifetime. To compare myself to a professional dancer would be like a first grader with a calculator comparing himself to Einstein.

In New Orleans at on
of the Triple Crown Event

It just doesn't fly. We all work with the talent we are given, and the dedication we choose to employ will get us as close as we can get to our own standard of beauty.

One of the trade-offs of dancing so many heats during the day at the comp is that sometimes I am just too tired and sore to get dressed again and go back to the ballroom to watch these great artists. But I console myself with the thought that even if I am curled up with icepacks and the companionable blither of TV, it is because I want to be able to dance my best the next day. I think the professionals would understand.

Try as I might to stay aloof and disconnected while I'm dancing, sometimes it is impossible not to come into contact with other dancers out on the floor. Dancing is a contact sport—don't let anyone try to convince you it is any more peaceful than rugby or football. With all the couples whirling around on the same floor, all strategizing to dance aggressively through the same space, there are collisions, and sometimes they are not pretty.

There is floor etiquette for managing a bump with another couple, depending on how hard it is. Generally, there is a quick apology before you continue dancing. While it is important for the judges to see dancers handle collisions gracefully and graciously, it is also crucial that dancers not lose the beat they are dancing to. After all, a heat is only a little more than a minute. Dancers have no spare seconds to squander trying to recoup a lost beat. You stop, "collect," and continue your routine, since there is a prescribed Line of Dance which all the other couples are following, too. If the collision was serious, though, you take more time to apologize off the floor once the heat is over.

The reason couples dance aggressively is that you are judged in part by your ability to dominate the floor. This means that to some degree graceful determination is rewarded. It is not polite, however, to dance into another couple's space for no reason other than to upset their flow. Most people cross paths purely accidentally and are aggressive only in the sense that they want to attract notice, not because they want to create trouble for their competitors. After all, no dancer would want to be caught by a judge doing anything unseemly.

That said, there is a certain amount of floor rage. Sometimes it seems like a collision couldn't have been anything but intentional, and in cases like that, grudges don't die easily. I've heard of instructors who remember for twenty years who cut them off on the floor. Although you're not supposed to curse or swear—it doesn't fit into the dignified façade a dancer is supposed to present—I have heard someone dancing by me mutter, "screw his hairy ass!"

I have seen collisions happen to other people many times. As for us, I have had to jump over other people's feet once or twice. I have been smacked in the face, and Angelo has not only been bumped but squeezed into corners by other couples. Other than that, we never collide. This is because of Angelo's sixth sense. The closest we have ever come to smash-up was one occasion when we were trapped in a corner that another couple was moving into. Without missing a beat, Angelo actually dipped us under the linked hands of the other couple. It happened so suddenly, so smoothly, I almost didn't realize it had happened at all, and it took me several moments afterward to process the whole scenario. I have never seen any other couple pull a move like that, but Angelo made it look like we had planned the whole thing with the other couple all along.

There are other incidents on the dance floor that remind me that dancing really is a contact sport, although these incidents are rare.

BOLERO

Among all my beloved dances, the Bolero is one of my favorites. It combines the elements of Smooth and Rhythm, the seduction and the storytelling, into one fantastic and incredibly romantic pageant. Bolero is a Rhythm dance, but it is the slowest of them, and for this reason the dreaded Cuban Motion is a little more manageable. I love it because it requires all the intense emotion of the Rhythm dances, but gives me the time to make them deliberate and deeply expressive.

I find myself smiling naturally during the Bolero, which is wonderful. This is a widespread phenomenon during Rhythm and Latin dances; everyone on the floor is smiling. For professionals, there are a vast multitude of facial expressions, most of them different masks of extreme sexual desire. I can't possibly aspire to those. But I've already stretched myself beyond what I thought possible for myself. So who knows?!

In the middle of the Bolero, a dance I love.

Angelo and I watched one showcase where full lifts were allowed when the professional female dancer cut herself with her shoe. A stream of blood was running down her leg while her partner swooped her over his shoulder. They kept on dancing through to the end.

There are also falls. Dancers can fall by getting caught in their dress or snagging a heel on another foot. Sometimes the long flowing sleeves can float up and cover their heads, causing severe directional problems. If the dance floor is uneven, or has distinct seams, it can become a deadly obstacle course. When teachers see this kind of floor, they quickly let the organizer know and and do their best to dance around the tricky areas.

Once, Angelo and I were inadvertently shoved by another couple, and I could feel Angelo tipping backwards. All my maternal instincts went into alert mode and I physically kept his 235-pound body from crashing to the floor (that's a lot of adrenalin from a 105-pound mom!). Afterward, Angelo chastised me, saying I should never do that again, that I would hurt myself. He was a professional, and could take care of himself. I told him once a mother, always a mother, and that I would not be able to obey him on this one.

Falls are not infrequent, and professional dancers know how to fall and get up again without hurting themselves by just rolling back onto their feet. Most dancers who take a tumble are professionals, since professionals dance more showily and less defensively. Amateurs are often more cautious. I once saw one of the great dancers fall fast and hard during a heat. Within five seconds he had a cloud of six other teachers around him, all helping him up and checking to see if he'd sustained any injury. He was fine, if blushed red beyond embarrassment. That the scene made me feel proud to be a part of this world, where competing professionals looked out for their rivals, working together like a team, a band of brothers.

Until New Orleans, I had been blessedly exempt from any kind of unexpected problems on the dance floor. There, though, I took a sharp heel on my right foot. It hurt like hell. I danced on through the end of that heat and another five heats after it. I was so focused on the dance that I actually didn't think much of the pain—until the dancing stopped.

When I got off the floor, I realized my foot was purple and swollen, even more swollen than I expect it to be after a long day of dancing. It also hurt a bit more than it usually does, but not enough to keep me and Bob from walking around the French Quarter a bit. At the levee, we watched a Mississippi steamboat roll into dock, full of music and tourists hoping to claim a bit of the Big Easy as theirs for a moment. We went back to the hotel for dinner, looking forward to an evening of Gold-level and Professional competition.

Angelo is unhappy with this picture, since I am not pointing my left toe correctly.

But as we tried to get up to leave the dinner table, I realized that I couldn't walk. A tendon in the arch of my right foot had taken a major blow.

Bob literally had to carry me back to our room, and we had to leave the comp the next day. As disappointed as I was that I hadn't been able to stay through the end or see a little more of New Orleans, I was even more worried that my injury might sideline me for a long time. It turned out that I was lucky and hadn't broken any bones—I was stuck with my foot up and iced for several days of rest, which was inconvenient but not exactly fatal.

I had learned a lesson, though: I couldn't take a single day of dancing for granted. There is danger in the world where you least expect it. During the thrills and stresses of competition, it is also easy to forget how much you love what you do. That handful of days when I couldn't dance at all reminded me how much I adore dancing and the way it makes my body feel. How lucky was I to have found something I loved this much! I knew that many people go through their entire lives never feeling this way about anything—I know, because I used to be one of them. The injury was bad for my foot, but good for my heart. During the year, I can't even remember how many times I heard the words echo in my mind, *Each day I get to dance is a blessing.*

While I was cooling my feet for several danceless days, I happened to be flicking through a copy of *Dancebeat*, a monthly professional ballroom newspaper to which I now subscribed. I glanced quickly over the page that listed the top ten dancers in each category (Pro Male, Pro Female, Top Male Teacher, and so on), knowing that the rankings were determined by points accumulated since the Ohio Star Ball. It occurred to me that now that I might actually start to recognize some of those top ten names, since I had met so many people over the course of the last four comps.

LEADER BOARD

Regional Super Star Leaders

Top Teacher

Delgado, Tony	9,924.00
Ermis, Ben	7,424.00
Isaac, Jose	7,040.50
Vance, Forrest	6,263.00

Top Studio

American Ballroom Center	10,368.00
Starlight Ballroom	4,640.50
Team Delgado	4,400.00
Champion Dancesport	3,091.00

Top Male Student

Mitchell, Lawrence	1,734.50
Wang, Ming	1,242.00
Kusumi, Gary	1,004.00
Seder, Jeffrey	998.00

Top Female Student

Hattori, Taeko	3,458.00
Johnston, Charlotte	3,205.00
Lee, Josie	2,805.00
● Raurell, Lydia	2,761.00

Student * Student

Pye, Wally & Pye, Lynn	518.00
Morrison, Donald & Morrison, Bonnie	284.50
Borchelt, Jim & Borchelt, Sherry	274.00
Dimailig, Carlos & Dimailig, Eleanor	266.00

Most Valuable Player Standing

A	Perkins, Ruthie [Ermis, Ben]	92.00
	Cap, Natalka [Brock, Mark]	75.00
	Mendicino, Healey [Yates, John]	68.00
B	Perkins, Ruthie [Ermis, Ben]	164.00
	Goddard, Joan [Johnston, Chris]	104.00
	Chapman, Starr [Vuyovich, Kelly]	90.00
C	Johnston, Charlotte [Dovolani, Tony]	145.00
	Drysdale, Jim [Hansen, Maria]	136.00
	Moore, Beverly [Geirsson, Ingvar]	134.00

Dancesport Superbowl © 2004

2004 DanceSport SuperBowl Series Calendar

November 2003

Nov 26-28	California Star Ball Championships	213-387-3232
TBA	Gator Classic	941-925-4655

December 2003

Dec 10-14	Southeastern States Dancesport Championships	888-684-7717
Dec 11-14	Holiday Dance Classic Championships	619-291-7722
Dec 31-Jan 4	Yuletide Ball	301-972-2416

January 2004

Jan 29-Feb 1	The Falls Premier Ball	905-735-7221
Jan 30-Feb 1	Northeastern Open Invitational	860-563-2623

February 2004

Feb 5-7	Global Grand Challenge	614-268-2255
Feb 12-15	California Open Championships	314-579-9700
Feb 12-14	La Classique DuQuebec	514-362-1181
Feb 22-24	Dancers Cup Circuit Grand Ball	636-227-7202
Feb 27-29	Indiana Challenge	219-322-5880

March 2004

Mar 2-6	Heritage Classic	954-757-5101
Mar 4-6	Vegas Show Down	714-520-9469
Mar 11-14	St Louis Star Ball	636-207-0755
Mar 26-28	Tri-State Challenge	772-468-2900
TBA	Texas Challenge Championships	281-564-9354

April 2004

Apr 2-4	San Francisco Open	650-366-0504
Apr 7-11	Southern States Dancesport Championships	888-684-7717
Apr 15-18	Wisconsin State Dancesport Championships	262-367-3367
Apr 16-18	Philadelphia Festival DanceSport Championships	856-546-5077
Apr 24-25	Stardust Ball	516-333-8928
Apr 29-May 1-2	Emerald Ball DanceSport Championships	800-851-2813
TBA	Boleros' Grand Assembly Dancesport	904-721-3399
TBA	Can-Am Dancesport Gala	905-822-2986
TBA	Michigan Dance Challenge	248-399-4651

May 2004

May 6-8	Atlanta Open	314-579-9700
May 13-15	Randy Ferguson's Dance Houston	281-935-9047
May 27-30	American Star Ball	609-518-2070
TBA	People's Choice Dancesport	480-473-1678

June 2004

Jun 10-13	Maryland Dance Championships	443-262-9120
Jun 11-13	San Diego Dancesport Championships	619-291-7722
Jun 17-20	Central Florida Heat	352-326-3833
Jun 17-20	Colorado Star Ball	303-412-1213
Jun 17-20	Yankee Classic	772-595-9547
Jun 18-20	Chicago Crystal Ball	773-267-3411
Jun 23-27	Millennium Dancesport Championships	813-681-9749
TBA	Sapphire Ball Championships	512-261-4772

July 2004

Jul 1-4	Desert Classic Dancesport Festival	310-544-1609
Jul 7-10	Twin Cities Open	952-892-0876
Jul 28-31	Volunteer State Dance Challenge	615-593-2491
Jul 30-Aug 1	International Grand Ball Championships	415-752-5658
TBA	Danse Montreal de danse sportive	514-354-2210
TBA	Virginia State Championships	281-856-9421

August 2004

Aug 3-8	FL State Dancesport Championships	888-684-7717
Aug 6-8	Summit Rockies DanceSport Championships	303-596-5644
Aug 12-14	Heart of America Championships	913-369-3204
Aug 19-24	Cincinnati Dancesport	513-281-5500
Aug 19-22	Nevada Star Ball	702-367-8194
Aug 26-28	Capital Dancesport Championships	203-978-1987
TBA	Midwest Invitational	248-343-8337
TBA	Empire State	516-586-1449

September 2004

Sept 15-18	Diamond Classic	954-757-5101
Sept 23-25	Cleveland Dancesport Challenge	216-292-7371
TBA	Constitution State Dancesport Championships	860-563-2623

October 2004

Oct 1-3	Southwestern Invitational	512-671-7952
Oct 7-9	First Coast Dancesport Championships	904-733-9219
Oct 13-16	Hotlanta Dance Challenge	770-592-9746
Oct 28-31	Grand National Dancesport Championships	954-227-1760
TBA	Golden State Challenge	310-544-8699
TBA	New Jersey State Open	609-518-2070

November 2004

Nov 5-7	Pacific Dancesport Championships	877-553-5735
Nov 10-14	Caribbean Dancesport Classic	973-448-4526
Nov 16-21	Ohio Star Ball Championships	614-848-7827

Indeed, I recognized a name under Top Female Students. It was my name, in 4th place! Me, listed with all those top dancers! Me, in 4th spot on the National Leader Board. Oh my.

Let me clarify what exactly "Top Female Student" is. Being in 4th on the Leaderboard by no means meant I was the 4th best student or even the 4th best female student in the country—no sir. There are hundreds of women who are much more talented and graceful than I am in my own category of Bronze, never mind in the Silver and Gold categories. Of course, most of us feel like cows compared to the professional dancers (which is okay with me—it is nice to have an ideal against which to compare my progress). What it does mean is that I had collected the fourth highest number of points in the NDCA DanceSport Series thus far in the year—by competing in as many heats as I could, placing as well as I could, and coming back resiliently to comp after comp.

Many students wouldn't even consider trying for the Top Student award. They have other priorities within a dance category, they don't have the time, they don't have the financial means, or it simply isn't their goal. But was it a goal that I, personally, could work towards?

To say I was caught by surprise wouldn't quite paint a picture of that moment. When I recovered use of my voice, I dialed Angelo as quickly as I could, and we were elated together. I had never dreamed of being so close to the top. What if. . . . Could I possibly. . . . Did I really stand a chance . . . ?

I made up my mind while I was on the phone with him. This was my year of If-Not-Now-Then-When? I was going to give it a shot. I was going to put every ounce of my being into making Top Female Student of the Year.

Chapter 7
PARTNERSHIP

Over the next three months, April to June, I visited six American cities in five different states for a total of twenty-three days of competitive dancing. We danced from the Philadelphia Festival to the Los Angeles Emerald Ball, to the Atlanta Open to the Central Florida Heat. Sometime during the rush, I turned fifty-five. Angelo and I were on a whirlwind tour, dedicated as we were now to racking up as many points at as many comps as possible. Every heat counted at this point.

We hadn't disclosed to anyone our goal to try to take Top Student. I didn't want to jinx our chances. I had seen what even a minor accident could do when I was injured in New Orleans, and how simple it was to be taken out of the running entirely. But no matter how vulnerable or incompetent one feels on the insides, proof of your competence will emerge. I had heard the idiom "success breeds success" before, but I had never personally understood what it meant. Now I was beginning to see that the more I won, the more I could win.

In April, I had been in 1st place, in May, 2nd. As of my twelfth comp, the Millennium Dancesport Championships in St. Petersburg, Florida, my scores had put me back on top of the National Leaderboard. That was when I realized exactly how much the pressure was on me to dance well. I was no longer an unknown fifty-five-year-old doing competitions for fun. I wasn't a "coulda been," I was a contender. My name this high on the Leaderboard at this point in the dance year was irrefutable. It was a public declaration.

Although my nerves were starting to ebb, the comps themselves didn't get any easier. This is because I was learning more about ballroom dance with every comp, and I was learning it fast. As with many pursuits, with dancing, the more you learn, the more you realize you still have to learn. Practice is not optional. I needed to keep up energy and momentum, physically and emotionally, every day. If I ever missed a day of practice, I felt like it took me a week to catch up again.

I told my friends—only semi-jokingly—that I was on Dance Sabbatical Year. When I made the decision to shoot for Top Student, I warned them that I probably wouldn't see as much of them for a while. Some were upset, but most were supportive and excited for me. This was a difficult but necessary trade-off; I would be practicing ballroom dance more intensely than I had ever done anything before.

In some ways it felt as though I had run away with my husband to join the circus. Or, perhaps more accurately, it felt as though we had become a three-person circus, me, Angelo, and my husband. Bob and Angelo were my two partners on this journey, each in their own distinct way.

Angelo, of course, was my ballroom partner. Ballroom dance is a wonderful lesson in partnership and cooperation, in seeing how important it is to be sensitive to the people around you who are working with you. Ballroom is an unusual art form in that there really aren't any solo performances; as a dancer, you are never alone on the floor. You are always with your partner, on whom you must be able to depend com-

*At the Manhattan DanceSpo\
comp we execute a Hesitatio\
in the International Foxtr*

pletely and implicitly. You must be able to trust your partner in a way you don't have to trust most people you'll ever meet. Ballroom partnership is a marriage of sorts, a business relationship as well as an emotional relationship and a friendship. It needs energy and humor, or it would feel too much like a job, and would never survive the fights and arguments.

Yes, there are fights on the road. Angelo and I would get sick of each other, or I would get tired of being told what to do. I knew he was my teacher and that I was really not much different from a child learning to walk, but as an adult woman, sometimes I just wanted things to work out my way. Angelo believed in my talent and ability, and usually I believed in his belief enough to make it work, but sometimes I got exhausted. In our case, our partnership was so strong that any argument we ever had was surmountable.

All partnerships have their idiosyncrasies, but one thing most successful partners have in common is they protect each other, trust each other, and have a lot of fun together. A good teacher, like Angelo, is a gentleman who will graciously see the lady through any kind of awkward situation.

For example, there is the issue of what is known as a "wardrobe malfunction." Most women have curves. I am not in this category. That does, however, give me the advantage of not having to worry about breast exposure. Ballroom dresses are made to accentuate the female figure, and sometimes they do not include enough defense mechanisms against all the exciting possibilities a full figure presents. When the "malfunction" happens, the male partner will instantaneously stand in front of the exposee and wait while she rearranges the situation. If rearrangement isn't possible, he will closely escort her from the floor.

Learning to work with Angelo meant learning to trust him in such a very personal space. The first time I bought a dress with an open back

Angelo and I warm up during our practice time at the Brooklyn comp. We are doing our Open American Tango entrance step.

was a horrible trauma for me. The second Angelo touched the bare skin in the correct place below my shoulder blade I shrieked and jumped back. It was very rude of me. No one but my husband had touched my bare skin in twenty-five years. It took me three tries to let Angelo get me into the dance frame, hand on my back, and even then I couldn't stand it.

Angelo told me not to worry, that when I got on the dance floor I would be too preoccupied with my dance steps and the judges to think about my back. He was right. But I also realize now that he wouldn't have been right if I hadn't already learned to trust him completely.

Angelo has a knack for alleviating stress with humor, and his antics kept the whole project worthwhile. I'm a really straight-and-narrow, polite person, so I am the perfect foil (not to mention target) for Angelo. He likes to lighten up practice by taking on a role in the studio. We greet each other in the morning for practice with a new salutation: *Salve! Howdy! Bonjour! Ciao, Baby! Hi!* I'm supposed to remember to stick out my sternum, instead of my neck, but sometimes I forget, and when I do, Angelo says I look like Marlon Brando in *The Godfather.* Every time I slip and jut out my neck, he starts his *Godfather* shtick. When I move my feet too fast, without enough grace, he says I look like the Lollipop Guild in the Munchkin scene in *The Wizard of Oz,* and he goes into his Muchkin shtick. When things get going too fast or slow during practice, he pretends to jump out the window. Whenever we're dancing in the studio and sirens go by outside, Angelo pretends to be a stripper!

At airports and hotels, Angelo walks me right into the men's room. Talk about bathroom humor. We dare each other a lot. Once, he started going up the down escalator in the airport in Atlanta—that's the steepest escalator in the world. I had to follow, of course. Neither of us lasted very

LYDIA

Favorite Car – Saab
Favorite Drink – water, don't drink alcohol
Favorite Rock Band – Rolling Stones
Favorite Dress Designer – Ralph, Armani, Cavalli
Best Friend – My husband, my sister.
Favorite Movie – *Gone with the Wind*, anything by Visconti and Busby Berkely, and anything with Fred Astaire dancing

ANGELO

Favorite Car – Porsche
Favorite Drink – beer, Diet Coke, Bacardi Limone
Favorite Rock Band – The Eagles
Best Friend – My wife, Sandra, and Bill, who likes me for who I am and is not judgmental. He is with Airforce Intelligence and travels the world protecting our country.
Fashion designer – Brioni, Canali, Hugo Boss
Favorite Movie – The Wizard of Oz

long, But it was a blast. We give each other a lot of grief. He gives me more than I give him. When he is being too serious or grumpy, I pretend to kick him in the balls.

Perhaps because of his training in theater, or his natural love of stardom, Angelo often gets the urge to entertain people in public. Angelo has a quirky and infectious sense of humor, from which he does not spare anyone who comes across his path.

Once, we stopped in front of the door of a very large homemade craft and gift store near the comp hotel in Ashville, North Carolina. We had noticed that the stately front door was hung with bells. I was commenting on how pretty they were when Angelo suddenly opened the door and announced to the assembled shoppers, "Hi, honey! I'm home!"

What's remarkable about Anglo's attitude is that he really doesn't mind if others don't find him funny, although they almost always do, because it is so obvious he gets much pleasure from his own jokes. One of his favorites is to step into a crowded elevator and politely say, "Twenty-second floor, please." There will be a three second pause and then laughter and confusion as the occupants realize that there are only eighteen floors in the hotel.

When you are a dance student, you get in the habit of being obedient to your teacher's voice and his gestures. So when we are in airports or train stations or subways, Angelo leads the way, by default. For an entire year (not to mention the subsequent years of our collaboration!) Angelo would tell me to go right—which I would do, only to turn around eight seconds later to find that he was walking in the opposite direction. He also likes to disappear suddenly, and then pop out from behind a pillar. I am always entertained, never annoyed. Plus, sometimes I get him back.

I happen to have excellent aim, with any object I pick up. Like the snowball with which I nailed Angelo in the snowstorm at the Greenbrier. There was also that time in the studio when he was teaching me how to shape my arms and hands by using a plastic cup. I got frustrated and he dared me to throw the plastic cup at him. Bad idea. I beaned him on the head.

One thing Angelo and I share is an inordinate amount of curiosity. This means we don't mind getting lost while trying to find a hotel or a dance studio in a new city. We like to explore, and our list of destinations actually includes some locales that are not sports bars.

When we were at a comp in St. Augustine, we finally took some time out to take in a few sights. I wasn't going to pass up the opportunity to see the Fountain of Youth! The heat was literally blistering that day, which meant we had the park to ourselves. I bought a bottle of Fountain of Youth Elixir, but I haven't drunk it to this day—maybe I'll have it on my 60th birthday. We also went to the historic Native American burial site, which gave Angelo the creeps. So we paid our respects and went on to the Crocodile/Alligator Zoo.

The zoo was home turf for me, since zoos are my husband's and my favorite tourist stops. Angelo was polite about it at first, smiling gently at my squawks of awe and fascination at all the prehistoric reptiles. At my suggestion we attended the zoo's show, which featured a trainer who got the gigantic crocs to jump up and bite a very large stick. That was when Angelo started to get antsy. I wasn't nervous, since I had read enough about crocs to know that if you get too close, you just have to poke it in the eye, then ram the stick down his gullet. Useful information, just in case.

The zoo also had a selection of exotic trees, two of which were particularly weird and a little bit spooky. I told Angelo to be careful.

"Don't touch them!" I whispered. "They'll bite you!" Angelo looked queasy and very quickly and quietly slunk away from them. It was a mistake for me to tell him later that I was only kidding—he got me back threefold.

Angelo, my ballroom partner, is in complete cahoots with my other cohort, my life partner: husband, Bob. I know for a fact that I would never have started competing if it hadn't been for their little machinations. "We Capricorns have to stick together," Angelo tells Bob. Yes, they are both Capricorns. I don't know much about the Zodiac, but I have a sneaking suspicion that in this case, at least, Angelo might be onto something.

"We Capricorns think alike," Angelo says. Bob and Angelo certainly both think they know what's best for me. "Be quiet and listen to your Capricorns," says Angelo.

The trouble is, they do know what's best for me—just ask them—and they each do everything in the world to take care of me, even when I want them to just leave me alone. But no dice. In their defense, they have gotten me this far. It was Bob who helped me realize how much I loved dancing—forced me to realize, really; practically dragged me kicking and screaming. For this, I am forever grateful to him. He has been a pillar of support at every step of the way, coaxing me through nerves, injuries, illnesses, and bouts of self-doubt. After twenty-five years of marriage, he knows me so well that he does often know what's better for me than I know myself. That doesn't mean it is always easy for me to go along with his advice.

Ballroom is a physical sport.
There's nothing like a good hug after
an hour of intense work!

Bob's style is a little different than Angelo's. He's much subtler. With Bob, I find myself going his way without realizing at what point he had convinced me. He never raises his voice. It's very clever of him. He masquerades as my cheerleader, when in fact I wouldn't be competing at all if he hadn't convinced me to compete by lulling me into submission.

On the road, Bob—who comes to comps as often as he can get away from work—acts as my manager and official photographer. He is, as I've mentioned, a lovely dancer himself, and it's always nice to have the opportunity to dance together during a "general dance," the social moments of the competitions. But Bob, bless him, is content and satisfied to let this be my show, all about me. He is patient with me through my worst moments and makes himself readily available to ensure things run smoothly.

I, for one, feel like every award I win is actually an award that Bob and I have won together. Quite honestly, without Bob, there *is* no Lydia.

While some women who have partially retired decide to become a scratch golfer, ride their horses every day instead of only on the weekends, to go on the bridge circuit, or start up their own businesses, I decided to dance. Without Bob's emphatic support, which meant daily encouragement, I would not, could not have taken even one step into this terpsichorean universe.

We have a rule that we are never apart for more than two weeks, and have kept this rule for thirty-one years. If Bob were to ask me to stop doing competitive ballroom dancing, for any reason, even without a reason, I would stop that second, no questions asked. He knows this.

Bob and I believe that to love each other fully is to encourage each other to do our work, and to nurture each other's souls. How can we hope to live and love without personal growth? He stayed with me

LYDIA

Favorite Color: Blue, Mother-of-Pearl

Favorite Music: Bach, Vivaldi, Bo Diddley

Favorite Food: PB&J on whole wheat, poached salmon, spinach, caviar, Caesar's salads

Favorite Sports Team: Yankees

Favorite Author: Tolstoy, Romain Roland, Dickens

Languages Spoken: rusty French, rustier Spanish, Op Language, NYC City Street talk

Sports Played: ballet, tennis, field hockey, lacrosse, basketball, softball, gymnastics

Hobbies: swimming, reading, playing the baroque recorder

BOB

Favorite Color: Red

Favorite Music: Philip Glass, Hawaiian slack key guitar

Favorite Food: Indian

Favorite Sports Team: Yankees

Favorite Author: Giovanni de Lampedusa, George MacDonald Fraser, Alan Furst, Larry McMurtry, Vladimir Nabakov, Ludwig Bemelmans, William Shakespeare, Donna Leon, Charles Dickens, Joseph Conrad, Robert Louis Stevenson, Fyodor Dostoevsky, Tom Wolfe, Christopher Buckley, Emily Dickinson, J.K. Rowling, F. Scott Fitzgerald, self

Languages Spoken: Italian, French, some English

Sports played: Golf, bicycling, tennis, backgammon

Hobbies: being with my wife, writing poetry, cigars

Bob and I dress up in theme for an evening at the Grand National Championships in Miani.

through my times of illness, and he is with me during my time of health. I trust that we will be together through all the seasons of our lives.

Angelo and his wife, Sandra, and Bob and I have a very happy friendship. When we all travel together, as we sometimes do to competitions, it is a merry time. The dance is our muse and our theme, and she has led us to discovering many new cities in the United States and abroad.

Bob and Angelo can shop for days together, for anything or nothing. We all love to sightsee, and walking on the beach after the comps in California

My husband, Bob, is my photographer as well as my dance manager and my true love. He took these shots during the American Smooth heats at our New York City comp.

After a number of heats are danced, all the competitors are called back onto the floor for placement awards.

...able full of the participation awards given out at our ...ooklyn comp. These delightfully whimsical statuettes were ...ery nice reminder that partnership takes many forms.

is one of our favorite activities, especially as we get to breathe fresh air, which is one commodity that does not exist in the dance ballrooms!

At Newport Beach the two Capricorns decided to become surfers, so we all went to the nearby surf shop (of which there are about ten per block) and they bought the whole shebang: a full body suit for Bob, a hip surfer bathing suit for Angelo, goggles, towels, bandanas—well, Bob bought the bandana; he is older than Angelo and not therefore not as sensitive to looking like an idiot. The two dudes approached those ten-foot high waves . . . well, they approached for a long time. Then they put their feet in the water. Expletives were audible over the roar of surf. That Pacific water is cold, it turns out! Remember we are all from Florida, home of the warm Gulf Stream. But those guys weren't going to let hypothermia or a death wave stop them. So, out came Angelo's hearing aid, on went Bob's bandana. I began to pray as the two men dove into the glacial world famous waves. Yes, they did dive through the waves, no, they did not attempt to body surf the ten-footers, yes, they did return, blue eyed and triumphant. They had a look of euphoria and profound relief. Then we went for an hour-long bicycle ride in one of those four-seater contraptions. For the guys, it was not hard looking at the California girls. We were all grooving to "California Dreaming."

We all play gin (in which Sandra and I play on a team together and we always win against the guys, ha ha). We all like to eat. Well, Angelo and Bob *really* like to eat. The search for the best BBQ ribs in town is a frequent quest, not to mention the quest for the best beers. Bob travels and works really, really hard at his own career. The times with Angelo and me on the road is a lot of work of another kind: mediating when Angelo and I decide we detest each other, or being my coach and shrink when I decide to quit competing. Otherwise, my dance world it is a wondrous distraction for him. It is such a great adventure to be on together.

CHAPTER 8
THE DISCIPLINE OF THE DANCE WORLD

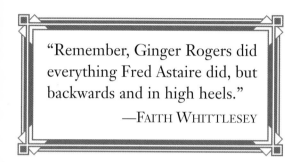

"Remember, Ginger Rogers did everything Fred Astaire did, but backwards and in high heels."

—FAITH WHITTLESEY

*I*n all the hullabaloo of the competition circuit, I couldn't forget that my body had become a utensil that needed to be cared for meticulously. It had to be fed, exercised, and stretched. I had to discover and experiment with "athletic" cuisine: protein for muscles, carbs for energy, bananas for potassium to prevent muscle cramping. I learned to drink power shakes, eat protein bars, and snack on nuts and peanut butter. My favorite fallback food became the ubiquitous Caesar salad, full of leafy greens and chicken for protein. I became a walking Caesar salad.

I had to try to build as much muscle and flexibility as I could—I became a mini body builder. After six months, none of my old jackets and shirts fit, because my shoulders had become broader.

You can imagine how thrilled I was the first time I realized that for a ballroom dancing comp I was going to be wearing heels for seven or eight consecutive hours. Furthermore, I would be spending these long hours on my feet—for all intents and purposes, running around in my heels.

If you have never danced before, you might think that my feet eventually got used to the pressure, toughened up against the high heels, and stopped hurting. You would be most woefully wrong. Halfway through a competition, my feet hurt so much a thought wanders across my mind—is today the day they fall off? I know they haven't actually fallen off yet, but is today the day? My feet get so swollen that if I take my shoes off to ice them mid-afternoon, I often have trouble fitting them back into the shoes afterwards.

It's not just *my* feet. All dancers, I can guarantee, have these same thoughts and pains, even the men (who have the luxury of thinking they have it rough without the actual experience of dancing in heels).

It's not only our *feet* that hurt, either. Our entire legs ache, not to mention the whole rest of our bodies. One of the areas a dancer works hardest to control is the abdomen, our core muscles that hold up our torsos and keep our lines flush from shoulder to toe. After eight hours of tightly isolating your stomach muscles, even your ribcage hurts.

There are also the arms. Have you ever tried standing still for five minutes with your arms straight out on either side of you? Go ahead, give it a shot. You think at first that it is going to be a piece of cake, but about two minutes into it you'll realize that it's not quite as easy as you first thought. Now imagine keeping your arms that way for hours, and you will know how our shoulders, backs, and chests burn at the end of a long day of heats.

I'll admit that arm pain is one area where the gentlemen have the short end of the stick. While the ladies get some reprieve with their arms, the men must have theirs up the entire time they are dancing, and they are frequently bearing at least some of their partners' body weight. There are, of course, the partial lifts as well, during which he is supporting a lot of his female partner's weight. For this, male dancers need both brute strength and true muscular endurance.

This is why dancers love ice. Ice is our best friend. There is so much ice at any given comp that we might as well be dancing on the South

American Cha-Cha Crossover.

*Right, Angelo ducks to avoid getting smacked
on the head from the couple behind us.*

Pole. We are caught up in the music, the steps, and the adrenalin when we are on the floor, but the moment we step off onto the carpet everything starts to burn.

I had never used an ice machine in a hotel room before I started dancing. I prefer to drink beverages at room temperature, thank you very much. Now that I've been on the comp circuit, though, I have come to appreciate the ice machine for all its chilling wonder. I carry around four star-spangled ice packs and fill them at the ice machines whenever I get a spare moment. At big comps, we have no trouble emptying ice machines. I know one teacher who brings two trash cans and fills them both, simply stepping in and submerging himself up to his thighs when he's off the floor.

In order to prepare ourselves for the intense workout that a competition is, dancers have to be very disciplined about their fitness and health. This actually happens naturally—you don't even notice as your heart gets stronger, you run out of breath less quickly, and your limbs turn to muscle. One woman I know lost forty pounds because of all the exercise. She was a lost soul when she first came into dancing—she was lonely, restless, had no self-confidence. When she discovered dancing and her sense of purpose, she transformed herself. She found her passion, her body, her community, her career—she actually ended up becoming an instructor.

No matter how old or what shape you are, dancing makes you younger and fitter. It was terrific to learn what my body could do. That famous statistic about the Viennese Waltz's being a better form of exercise than running three times a week is a favorite of mine, but cardiovascular fitness isn't the only perk of dancing. Studies suggest that ballroom dance contributes to preventing Alzheimer's, and I believe it. Remembering all the steps, each of which has its own name and special execution, is a mental workout for me.

*Angelo and I fly across the flo
in the International Viennese Wal
Here, we execute swirli
Right Box tur*

Physical conditioning is not the only discipline in the dance world, though. There is also the getting up at the crack of dawn to get ready aspect. I was used to early rising because of all the running around I used to do as a single mother, but I know some other dancers have a little more trouble with this. To be perfectly honest, though, I've never had my hair done before 6:45, which is practically last call. Call me a wimp. Some women have their hair done at 4:00 AM. Good for them.

On the road, we set our alarms for 5:00 AM or earlier. The hairstyles, which have to be both ornate and tough enough to withstand hours of wild movement, take a good deal of time, as does make-up application and dressing in the complicated costumes.

Bronze students are at the bottom of the ladder, since we have yet to prove ourselves and graduate to Silver, then Gold. Because of this, Bronze students have to get up the earliest at any comp. We are the ones crowding the dressing rooms getting our hair done at six in the morning, because we are going to be the ones that have to be out on the floor first, at 7:00 AM— looking like we have been awake and in eveningwear for hours.

I set out everything the night before: matching earrings, hair bows, ornaments, clean tights. I brush the suede soles of all my shoes, removing rhinestones, feathers, and dust from the previous day of dancing. I make sure the heels of all my pumps still have their heel protectors intact and not too worn down; otherwise, I must replace them. I lay my costumes over the backs of chairs so the skirt and fringe have time to breathe overnight. You are docked points for any sloppy appearance—tousled hair, smudged shoes, runs in stockings, anything at all out of place. There are even rules about your nails—fingernails should be long and pearly polished; toenails should be red. Yes, the judges do notice!

Even with the greatest care taken, there are always some wardrobe

VIENNESE WALTZ

Like the Waltz, the Viennese Waltz has the honor of being the oldest among the ballroom dances, dating back to the second half of the 18th century. It was first frowned upon as a provocative dance—because women's ankles were exposed—and all but forgotten. It is so irresistible, though, that society eventually came around. It has always been one of the most popular dances and has had music specially written for it by some of history's most famous composers.

The dance follows a fast triple time. Like the Waltz, the beats come in neat threes, but unlike the Waltz, the Viennese Waltz is a swirl of constant movement. It is the most aerobic dance, and also the dance in which you feel the most like part of an ensemble with all the other competitors. Because of the fast movement, the Line of Dance becomes especially important, and it is a marvel to be on the floor spinning in perfect cooperation (in theory!) with all the other couples.

The Viennese Waltz is just pure joy. This particular dance came the most easily to me. It is all made up of spins and runs, left and right turns, a wild, giddy dance that requires quick foot work and much physical endurance. Dancing it with a group of competitors is an adventure! All the couples are doing essentially the same steps all at the same time, swooping around the dance floor at a very fast speed. It is like being on or becoming part of a carousel in which the horses really are running—presumably without hitting one another. The women's dresses all whirl, whirl, whirl in this dance. When it is performed by professionals it is absolutely magical.

The rule in all dancing is that you breath through your smile, but this was the first dance in which I learned to smile totally, from within, no mask needed.

casualties over a long day of competition. All day long, dancers wipe, kick, or pick up all the feathers, rhinestones, earrings, and hairpins that have fallen off during preceding heats. One of my dancer friends had her shoe come off during a heat. She just kept dancing. Since she had several heats in a row, she had to finish them with one bare foot. Happily, the judges didn't notice. I almost wish they had, so they could have admired how well she danced under duress.

Hair is a serious business. As with just about every other component of competitive ballroom dance, there are strict regulations for hair design. It must fit the appropriate style category and be unique to the dancer, while being able to withstand spins, drops, perspiration, and sometimes several nights of sleep at the busiest comps. Basically, it needs to be stuck together with enough pins and hairspray to survive a hurricane.

The only reliable hairdressers are current or former dancers, a squad of whom are hired to work at most dance competitions. Some women book their hair appointments months in advance to make sure there will be someone who has time to treat them on their competition days.

I'm profoundly grateful for these hairdressers. I have a very small skull—I'm a bit of a peahead, in fact—so if I don't manage to bulk my hair up I look out of proportion on the floor. My hair is skinny and long, and I'm pretty pathetic at doing my own hair into anything other than a wispy ponytail or an old lady bun. The hairdressers, however, are old pros and seem to have no such problems. One woman has called my hair "cotton candy" because it's so easy to work with (wish I felt the same!). Those miracle-working hairdressers are able to produce wonderful, tall concoctions of swirls, coils, and curves, all in twenty minutes or less. My bangs are my substitute for Botox, since they so cleverly hide the "wisdom lines" on my forehead.

The hairdressers can also do make-up, but I prefer to do my own so that I can use my own products. I wasn't used to heavy dramatic make-up at first, but after some trial and error I eventually found the product combination that will stand up pretty well to the test of five hours of intense dancing. Obviously, the mascara, eyeliner, and base must be waterproof (Angelo is not the only dancer who sweats, I promise you).

There's an adage that says you can never be too tan on the dance floor, and a lot of women apply self-tanner to their bodies and face. That's a little messy for my taste, and requires higher maintenance. I prefer to wear tan colored tights instead.

Over the course of this cramped early-morning hour and a half, we have eaten, stretched, pressed our hair and shaped it, and layered on a whole second face of make-up. There is a mass exodus from the dressing room to the ballroom when that first heat approaches. The sight of hundreds of women silently rushing through the lobby of a hotel in iridescent colors and sparkling rhinestones is both normal and lovely, like a great flutter of giant butterflies.

I've overheard a more sarcastic interpretation of this river of satin and glitter and chiffon. Is there a hint of desperation about a herd of menopausal women determined to hang onto a semblance of beauty and womanhood with this pageant of acute femininity? An overly blatant howl for sex, for love, or simply for attention? Many of my fellow competitors in my age group are semi-retired, and many are lonely, having lost their spouses or partners to death, illness, or other women. Many have seen their children grow up and leave the nest. What will they do with their lives?

The unfairness of this interpretation stings me, and not only because I

count myself as one of the maligned. What all these costumed women have done—every single one of them—is make the decision to Never Give Up. They have committed their energy and their time (which, as we all know, gets more precious as we get older) to learning something new—learning how to dance, how to compete, how to become an athlete, how to give the best of their best to see what their minds and hearts can achieve. For those of us who came into ballroom only in our middle age, dancing isn't about refusing to grow old. It's simply about refusing to stop growing.

Furthermore, the dance world is rarely lonely. In it, I have found a community of people who love the same thing I do. The feeling of being on the floor with twenty other couples, all of us trying to do our best, is exhilarating. We are all looking for excellence together, and to a soundtrack of lovely music.

It is an optimistic world, too, because we are always progressing. The spirit of self-cultivation and graciousness that is the backdrop for the whole sport means that in competition, no one comes out disappointed, as long as they are going in with their heart in the right place. Although there are prizes and awards, there are no losers. I compete against and for an ideal. On our paths, there are sometimes valleys, obstacles, plateaus, months where you feel you will never make it to the next stage, but somehow you do, moving ahead and beyond. The joy, the challenge—and also the agony—is always seeking to be a better dancer.

In the dance world, we don't say "Break a leg," like stage actors do. We say, "Dance well."

Chapter 9
EYES ON THE PRIZE

$\mathcal{T}$he NDCA DanceSport Series is a nationwide competition circuit that divides the United States up into six geographical dance regions. According to NDCA rules, pro-am couples are awarded 1000 bonus points at the end of the year at the Ohio Star Ball if they manage to compete in all six regions. Angelo and I had our work cut out for us.

The next three months, leading up to my second Ohio Star Ball, took us to the Southwestern Invitational in Dallas; the First Coast Classic DanceSport Championships in Jacksonville; the New Jersey State Open in East Rutherford; the Grand National in Miami Beach; and the Caribbean DanceSport Classic in San Juan, Puerto Rico. In the course of forty-five days, from September 23 to November 7, I danced twenty-two days of competitions. Every day was packing, unpacking, repacking, hauling three suitcases of clothes, shoes, make-up through new airports, cabs, rental cars, hotels, accents, and weather. It was a blast.

My trip across America was full of lovely and colorful personalities. In Phoenix, I met a widower who had been married to his wife for 49 years. He told me the story of how he had started taking dance lessons six decades ago in order to impress his future wife. "I met her for the first time at a dance party," he told me. Instead of asking her to dance, he had confessed that he couldn't, but she insisted they give it a shot, anyway. "We danced three steps," he told me, "and she said, 'Let's sit down and keep talking.' We got married anyways." They took dancing lessons together for many years. "I know she would have wanted me to keep dancing," he said, and I felt a lump in my throat. I never met his late wife, but I think he was right. "Plus," he added, "it's not so bad being surrounded by so many beautiful women!"

There is also the gang of gentleman teachers who play poker together in the evenings on the road when all the dancing is over. They give each other a lot of grief over poker, the kind of razzing you only give your good friends. Sometimes they forget that ballroom and their card games don't overlap, and start talking about the ongoing game during dance heats. Whenever they got to be too wild for me, I would clap my hands over my ears, mutter, "Guy stuff! I am out of here!" and remove myself quickly.

Fortunately, I was always rewarded for my crazy schedules and hectic traveling. The ballroom dance industry is delightfully fond of prizes. At each NDCA comp, the top twenty point earners are given a prize—a special pin—and a credit voucher toward next year's comp. Of course, there are the prizes for 1st, 2nd, and 3rd places in each heat. Then there are other awards for categories, such as the Top Student award or Best Overall Student.

The prizes also include participation awards that are given to all those who dance at the competition. As Woody Allen said, "Eighty percent of success is showing up." The dance world recognizes this, and acknowledges with these awards the amount of effort and work it has taken each student to take up the challenge and show up for the competition. They are particularly lovely, often a statue of a couple dancing. Their significance is profound to me, as they are a tactile, permanent

Angelo and I review the dance catalogue at the Dallas comp before going on for our Smooth set.

representation of the ephemeral moment of the dance itself.

This is why I came away from some of the comps with a trove of treasures. To me, every award is precious. Every little paper or star button is visible proof of achievement. I save them all.

I have a habit of curtseying when I receive an award. Although this is not the norm, I just can't seem to break myself of the habit. My curtseying is instinctive, as I had been taught to curtsey as a child at home and in school. Besides, I've always felt that I owed the judges some visible sign of respect and thanks for rewarding me. In all my time on tour, I've only met two other dancers who do this.

By the time Angelo and I reached this last stretch in September and October, the Leaderboard was still listing me in first place. Contrary to relaxing and feeling pleased with myself, I knew that now was the time I needed to keep the pedal to the metal. Many of the other Female Amateurs were improving just as much as I was over the course of their time on the road, and I had set everyone else on the Leaderboard a potentially attainable goal with my score. I would need to push myself even harder to maintain first place. I needed to keep fighting, no matter how sore my body was. I had to drive self-doubt from my mind and keep putting one foot in front of the other, as perfectly as possible.

I memorized two mini-mantras to help me along. The first is by Emerson: "Without ambition, one starts nothing. Without work, one finishes nothing. The prize will not be sent; you have to win it."

The second is by Billie Jean King: "Champions adjust. Pressure is a privilege." The more I competed, the more I realized this was true. I reminded myself daily how privileged I was.

It was in Puerto Rico, during my last comp before the Ohio Star Ball, that my luck ran out. I came down with the flu—a nasty version of it—and then, for icing on the cake, I got an inflamed Achilles tendon as a side effect from the antibiotics. There was no way around it—there would be no more dancing. I flew home from San Juan early and sulked in bed. I was miserable, frustrated, and genuinely agonized that I couldn't dance.

I believe that the human body was designed for movement. This is one thing I learned during the course of my wild first year of dancing. My body was happier when it was moving, working, flexing itself, testing its limits. This is why getting sick was doubly offensive to me. No only couldn't I compete, I couldn't even dance.

Over the course of the weeks I had to spend away from Angelo's dance studio, I had ample time to reflect. I realized that dancing had become my life. I couldn't bear the thought of never dancing again. What if my Achilles tendon never healed? How would I ever cope? What would I do? It was unbearable to pass those many weeks without even going to the studio. My daily world had become alien to me—I belonged on the dance floor! At fifty-five years old, I had finally found my place in life—and I couldn't get there. Patience is a very difficult virtue to practice.

My dear husband, Bob, nursed me back to health during this dance-less time. With his unflagging devotion and support, I got myself back together so I could at least attend the Ohio Star Ball, even though I still could not dance.

When Ohio came around again in mid-November, my foot was still in a brace. I hadn't danced in what seemed like months. Yet when the points were tallied up, the Leaderboard still said I was in first place. Apparently I had accumulated enough points during my whirlwind tour that none of the other dancers could catch up.

Even so, at the end of the ball, when the prizewinners were named

After competing in a Standard Open Championship dance in Dallas, we are lined up awaiting the judge's results. The last couple called wins 1st place. It is a moment loaded with tension.

With Sam Sodano, ballroom dance's godfather.
When he said, "Well, Lydia, you did it," it was
the highest compliment I had ever received.

and my name was called for Top Female Student, I still didn't believe it had actually happened. I was in an anxious daze, and on some level I was waiting for the other shoe to drop. Did I deserve this? *Yikes.*

How was I going to get to my feet, in front of so many people, without even my dance costume on? I felt vulnerable and exposed and shy. This was much harder than getting up to dance a heat. This time, it was just me, Lydia, a novice Bronze, with all those champion dancers and judges looking at me. I couldn't move from my chair. I was absolutely terrified to my core.

Angelo took my hand. "Come now," he said. I heard his voice, and, ever in my obedient student habit, I put myself into dancing posture. I put one foot in front of the other, with only a slight limp.

Sam Sodano smiled at me and handed me the trophy. "Well, Lydia, you did it," he said, and gave me a hug.

It was the highest compliment I ever received. *I did it.* In those three words, I realized I had become a different person. There was no way of refuting this award. No one could take it away from me—including, and most of all, myself. All my doubts about the steps, all the months of stretching and icing and training, all the hours of willing myself to go for broke, to do or die, of facing my fears—so many fears!—and reaching beyond my wildest dreams, all of it was over, and I had come out on top. I did it.

It was an emotion I had never experienced before. It was a strange feeling, some kind of rare validation. It was also a feeling of completion, freedom to succeed, to trust myself, and to have, well, a ball.

Also, for the first time in my life, I stayed up until three in the morning. That was when the very last awards were given out. It turned out that staying up was worth it.

Sam had been watching and judging me all year. He also made a special award in my honor, one that had never been given out before, because no student had ever done what I'd done this year. No one else in the United States had ever begun as a novice Bronze dancer and made it to the top of all the other female students—over three thousand of us—in the course of one year.

Of course, it's far from over. I may have gotten myself to the top of the Leaderboard, won Top Student, and been named Rookie of the Year. Now I just have to conquer Bronze, Silver, and Gold, and then who knows? Maybe become a champion. I can't wait. Bring it on. *Showtime!*

A teacher once told me you should approach dancing the same way you approach your life. I dance with gratitude. Dancing is a celebration of life.

Two awards! One for Top Female Student of the Year and one for Rookie of the Year. I am dazed and thrilled and full of gratitude.

ACKNOWLEDGMENTS

*F*or the making of this book (and the year of my life that inspired it), I owe my most genuine thanks to Angelo and Sandra Caruso, Penny Blatt, Vicki Rogers, Dennis Stewart, Peter Mayer, and Juliet Grames, without whom this book could not have been written. I would also like to add a personal note of thanks to each of the competition Organizers who hosted me over the year I've remembered here, and I hope I have not neglected any of these wonderful people. They are, in chronological order: Sam Sodano, Pete Taylor, Eddie Simon, Safwat Gerges, Gary McDonald, Esther and David Don, Debbie Avalos, Sarwat and Julia Kaluby, John DePalma, Marianne Nicole, Eddie Ares, Nancy Senner, Glenis Dee Creger, Andy and Sandy Fortuna, Elaine Green, Rosendo Fumero, Kathryn Schaffer, Danny Villavicencio, Jami Josephson, Jose and Beatrix Issaac, Michael Chapman, John Moldthan, Peter and Cassandra Schneider, Kelly Vuyovich, Ron and Karla Montez, Dan and Rebecca Messager, Randy and Audra Ferguson, Paul Jack, Judy Nixon, Forrest Vance, David Kloss, Brian and Kristy McDonald, Tetsu Kezuka, Chieko Yamamoto, John Kimmins, Wayne and Donna Eng, Wendy Johnson, Mary Murphy, Larry and Dianne Dean, Lisa Bentley, Linda Doyle, Keith Todd, Didio Barrera, Dan Sullivan, Yolanda Vargas, Paul Jack, Judy Nixon, Tania Giramella, Dennis and Jackie Rogers, Olga Bogdanov, Natalia and Andre Paramanov, Dawn Soeni, Dierdre Baker, Andrea Ringgold, Reed Miles, and David Innis

Here is a complete list of National Dance Council of America dance competitions. If you are interested in attending any of them, please get in touch with the organizer(s) listed. For more information on the comps, go to ndca.org.

NORTHEASTERN OPEN DANCESPORT INVITATIONAL
Stamford, CT
Ron & Lee Cote
TEL: (860) 529-5111 FAX: (860) 529-5222
Email: Mambo2341@aol.com
http://www.neodancesport.com

NASHVILLE STARZ DANCE SPECTACULAR
Nashville, TN
David Hamilton
TEL: (615) 828-4583
Email: smoothchamp@tds.net
http://www.nashvillestarz.net/

WINTER BALL
White Sulphur Springs, WV
Elaine Green, Ed and MaryAnne Foss
TEL: (513) 742-6262 FAX: (513) 742-6269
Email: elaine.green@fuse.net
http://www.winterball.net

MAGNOLIA DANCESPORT CHALLENGE
Memphis, TN
Kelly Vuyovich
TEL: (601) 818-4301 FAX: (601) 261-0265
Email: kdilluminations@aol.com
http://www.magnoliadancechallenge.com

MARYLAND DANCESPORT CHAMPIONSHIPS
Bethesda, MD
Glenis Dee Creger
TEL: (443) 262-9120 FAX: (443) 262-9121
Email: marylanddancesport@msn.com
http://www.marylanddancesport.com

FLORIDA SUPERSTARS
Tampa, FL
Michael Chapman & John Moldthan
TEL: (863) 668-9668 FAX: (863) 688-3012
Email: michchp9@aol.com
http://www.floridasuperstarsdancesport.com

BOLEROS GRAND ASSEMBELY DANCESPORT COMPETITION
Jacksonville, FL
Ralph Ramirez & Billy Fajardo
TEL: (904) 721-3399 FAX: (904) 721-0301
Email: boleros10131@aol.com
http://www.boleros.cc

CALIFORNIA OPEN DANCESPORT CHAMPIONSHIPS
Irvine, CA
Debbie Avalos Kusumi
TEL: (520) 219-4555 FAX: (520) 219-3855
Email: CaOpen@aol.com
http://www.californiaopen.com

EASTERN U.S. DANCESPORT CHAMPIONSHIPS
Boston, MA
Mark & Dawna Nocera and Bill Morganti
TEL: (877) 883-8732 or (617) 512-2828
FAX: (877) 883-8732
Email: dance@easterndancesport.com
http://www.easterndancesport.com

HERITAGE CLASSIC DANCESPORT CHAMPIONSHIPS
Asheville, NC
Viva Dance Promotions (Colin & Joy Hillary)
TEL: (954) 757-5101 FAX: (954) 757-5103
Email: VivaDanPro@aol.com
http://www.theheritageclassic.com

INDIANA CHALLENGE DANCESPORT COMPETITION
Merrillville, IN
Tim & Sue Bourget
TEL: (219) 322-8381 FAX: (219) 227-8192
Email: ssds@jorsm.com
http://www.indianachallenge.com

NEW YORK DANCE FESTIVAL
New York, NY
Michelle Officer & Edward Simon
TEL: (212) 665-4343 FAX: (212) 665-4343
Email: info@nydancefestival.com
http://www.nydancefestival.com

VEGAS SHOWDOWN
Las Vegas, Nevada
Maria Hansen & Mikal Watkins
TEL: (949) 633-8727 / (714) 401-9091
Email: vegasshowdown@yahoo.com
http://www.vegasshowdown.com

CITY LIGHTS BALL
San Jose, CA
Glenn Weiss & Barbara Gore
TEL: (650) 223-4950 (Glenn), (650) 544-6655 (Barbara)
FAX: (567) 661-9265
Email: weiss.glenn@gmail.com
http://www.citylightsball.com

ST LOUIS STAR BALL CHAMPIONSHIPS
St Louis, MO
Suzanne & David Nyemchek & Steve Brockman
TEL: (636) 207-0755 FAX: (636) 207-0782
Email: JustDancing@day-light.com
http://www.stlouisstarball.com

MUSIC CITY INVITATIONAL
Nashville, TN
Tango Ltd. of Tennessee, Inc. (Jim Peters and Lawrence Elkin)
TEL: (615) 352-1155 FAX: (615) 356-0127
Email: mcinvitational@comcast.net
http://www.nationaldanceclubs.com
March 20-22, 2009

TRI-STATE CHALLENGE
Stamford, CT
Esther & David Don
TEL: (772) 468-2900 FAX: (772) 468-2900
Email: tri-state.challenge@usa.net
http://www.tristatechallenge.com

UNITED STATES NATIONAL AMATEUR DANCESPORT CHAMPIONSHIPS
Provo, UT
Brigham Young University
TEL: (801) 422-4623 FAX: (801) 422-0451
Email: Curt_Holman@byu.edu
http://byunationals.com/

SOUTHERN STATES DANCESPORT CHAMPIONSHIPS - 36th Annual
New Orleans, LA
Dance Consultants, Unlimited Inc. (Larry & Dianne Dean)
TEL: (888) 684-7717 / (941) 753-7940
FAX: (941) 753-7948
Email: deansofdance@aol.com
http://www.sostatesdance.com
E-mail address for Larry and Dianne Dean is:
deansofdance@aol.com

TEXAS CHALLENGE DANCESPORT
Houston, TX
Peggy Heeney Papineau & Phillip Stephens
TEL: 713-266-0066
Email: benoit.papineau@videotron.ca
http://www.txchallenge.com

SAN FRANCISCO OPEN DANCESPORT CHAMPIONSHIPS
San Francisco, CA
Rex Lewis, Stephan & Denise Krauel
TEL: (650) 366-0504 FAX: (650) 366-0504
Email: info@sfopen.com
http://www.sfopen.com

MICHIGAN DANCE CHALLENGE
Dearborn, MI
Mark Brock
TEL: (248) 561-7711 FAX: (248) 336-2543
Email: michigandancechallenge@comcast.net
http://michigandancechallenge.com/

WISCONSIN STATE DANCESPORT CHAMPIONSHIPS
Milwaukee, WI
Dan & Rebecca Messenger
TEL: (262) 367-1206 FAX: (262) 367-3367
Email: dancetrends@mindspring.com
http://www.wiscstatedancechamp.com

PHILADELPHIA FESTIVAL & ATLANTIC COAST DANCESPORT CHAMPIONSHIPS
Int'l Airport Marriott Hotel - Philadelphia, PA
Sandra & Andy Fortuna
TEL: (856) 546-5077, (856) 869-0010
FAX: (856) 546-0952
Email: phillyfestival@comcast.net
http://www.phillyfestival.net

EMERALD BALL DANCESPORT CHAMPIONSHIPS
Los Angeles, CA
Wayne & Donna Eng
TEL: (702) 256-3830 FAX: (702) 256-4227
Email: wayne@dancevision.com
http://www.emeraldball.com/

INTER-STATE DANCESPORT CHALLENGE
Washington, DC
Rickey Geiger & Robert Woods
TEL: (703) 938-2709 FAX: (703) 938-2709
Email: GeigerDance@aol.com

GREAT RACE SPORTS FESTIVAL - BALLROOM DANCESPORT COMPETITION
Notre Dame, IN
The Great Race, Inc. - Ron Schmanske, CEO /
Nichy & Lisa Vegas (Neeli Productions)
TEL: (216) 577-6952 FAX: (574) 293-8324
Email: wow@michiana.org
http://www.grdsport.net

ATLANTA OPEN
Atlanta, GA
Debbie Avalos, Sarwat Kaluby & Sam Sodano
TEL: (520) 219-4555 FAX: (520) 219-3855
Email: atlopen@aol.com
http://www.atlantaopen.com

DANCING A LA CARTE CHAMPIONSHIPS
Springfield, MA
David Rosinski & Jean-Marc Generoux
TEL: (413) 538-7991 or (413) 519-2435
FAX: (413) 538-7991
Email: dancingalacarte@aol.com
http://www.dancingalacarte.com

AMERICAN STAR BALL CHAMPIONSHIPS
East Rutherford, NJ
American Star Productions, Inc. (Pete Taylor)
TEL: (302) 221-0331 FAX: (302) 221-0311
Email: info@crystaldansport.com
http://www.americanstarball.com

PEOPLE'S CHOICE DANCESPORT COMPETITION
Phoenix, AZ
Forrest Vance
TEL: (480) 473-1678 FAX: (480) 473-1678
Email: FVANCE1@AOL.COM

RANDY FERGUSON'S DANCE HOUSTON
Houston, TX
Randy Ferguson & Rosendo Fumero
TEL: (281) 392-1042 / (832) 236-9090
FAX: (281) 935-9047
Email: randyfdancehouston@yahoo.com

SAN DIEGO DANCESPORT CHAMPIONSHIPS
San Diego, CA
Wendy Johnson, Wayne Eng & Chris Johnston
TEL: (702) 256-3830 FAX: (702) 256-4227
Email: wayne@dancevision.com
http://sandiegodancesport.com/

CHICAGO'S CRYSTAL BALL DANCE COMPETITION
Chicago IL
Ron & Karla Montez
TEL: (1 877) RMONTEZ (766-6839)
FAX: (520) 744-6272
Email: rondance@comcast.net
http://www.chicagocrystalball.com

COLORADO STAR BALL
Denver,CO
Richard & Jennifer Booth
TEL: (303) 412-1213 FAX: (303) 412-8231
Email: info@coloradostarball.com
http://www.coloradostarball.com

YANKEE CLASSIC & NEW ENGLAND DANCESPORT CHAMPIONSHIPS®
Cambridge, MA
John & Cathi Nyemchek
TEL: (845) 268-6368 FAX: (845) 267-2623
Email: TheYankeeClassic@aol.com
http://www.theyankeeclassic.com/

CENTRAL FLORIDA HEAT COMPETITION
Daytona Beach, FL
Jose & Beatrix Isaac
TEL: (352) 326-3833 FAX: (352) 728-5670
Email: CFHDancesport@aol.com
http://www.starlightdancesport.com

MILLENNIUM 2000 DANCESPORT
St Petersburg, FL
Michael Chapman
TEL: (863) 668-9668 FAX: (863) 688-3012
Email: michchp9@aol.com
http://www.m2dance.com

SAPPHIRE DANCESPORT CHAMPIONSHIPS
Austin, TX
Connie Paley & Fonzie Zapata
TEL: (512) 261-4772 / 845-3776 (Cell)
FAX: (512) 261-4769
Email: sapphiredancesport@yahoo.com
http://sapphiredancesport.com

MANHATTAN DANCESPORT CHAMPIONSHIPS
Brooklyn, NY
Gary & Diana McDonald and Avi Kafri
TEL: (973) 276-1170 FAX: (973) 276-1430
Email: info@manhattandancesport.com
http://www.manhattandancesport.com

IMPERIAL STAR CHAMPIONSHIPS
Cherry Hill, NJ
Wayne & Donna Eng
TEL: (702) 256-3830 FAX: (702) 256-4227
Email: wayne@dancevision.com
http://www.northamericandancesport.com

TWIN CITIES OPEN BALLROOM COMPETITION
Bloomington, MN
Megamarc, Inc. (Scott & Amy Anderson)
TEL: (952) 892-3650
Email: megamarc@frontiernet.net
http://www.twincitiesopen.com

DESERT CLASSIC DANCESPORT FESTIVAL
Palm Desert, CA
Igor & Irina Suvorov
TEL: (714) 536-0387 FAX: (714) 536-8797
Email: isuvorov@aol.com
http://www.DesertClassicDanceSportFestival.com

VIRGINIA STATE DANCESPORT CHAMPIONSHIPS
Reston, VA
Virginia State Championships, Inc. (Rosendo Fumero & Kathryn Schaffer)
TEL: (281) 856-9421 FAX: (281) 859-7398
Email: ICANTANGO@aol.com
http://www.dancesportchampionships.com

VOLUNTEER STATE DANCE CHALLENGE
Nashville, TN
David Medeiros
TEL: (615) 593-2491 FAX: (615) 331-9329
Email: DuDance@aol.com
http://www.volstdancechallenge.com

INTERNATIONAL GRAND BALL CHAMPIONSHIPS
San Francisco, CA
Stephan & Denise Krauel
TEL: (650) 366-0504 FAX: (650) 366-0504
Email: info@internationalgrandball.com
http://www.internationalgrandball.com

FLORIDA STATE DANCE SPORT CHAMPIONSHIPS
Sarasota, FL
Dance Consultants, Unlimited Inc. (Larry & Dianne Dean)
TEL: (888) 684-7717 / (941) 753-7940
FAX: (941) 753-7948
Email: deansofdance@aol.com
http://www.flstatedance.com

SEATTLE STAR BALL
Seattle, WA
Robert & Monique Hrouda and William Reneaud
TEL: (206) 361-8239 or (425) 255-6122
FAX: (206) 365-5884
Email: organizer@seattlestarball.com

EMPIRE STATE DANCESPORT CHAMPIONSHIPS
Manhattan, NY
Safwat Gerges & Edward Simon
TEL: (212) 942-3123 FAX: (212) 942-3123
Email: edwardsimon3@aol.com
http://www.esdsc.com

HEART OF AMERICA CHAMPIONSHIPS
Kansas City, MO
LeRoy & Ginny Walters
TEL: (913) 369-3204 FAX: (913) 845-2255
Email: HofAmerica@aol.com
http://www.hoadancesport.com

NEVADA STAR BALL CHAMPIONSHIPS
Las Vegas, NV
Brian & Susan Puttock, Hilda Lanza
TEL: (702) 367-8194 FAX: (702) 367-8194
Email: MIMOTA@aol.com
http://www.nevadastarball.com

CINCINNATI DANCESPORT FESTIVAL
Sheraton Hotel, Cincinnati Airport - Cincinnati, OH
Eleanor Lachman
TEL: (513) 281-5500 FAX: (859) 781-3471
Email: Information@CincinnatiDancesport.com
http://cincinnatidancesport.com

CAPITAL DANCESPORT CHAMPIONSHIPS
Washington, DC
John DePalma & Marianne Nicole
TEL: 1 (866) 345-5154 FAX: 1 (740) 969-4457
Email: capdance@optonline.net
http://www.capitaldancesport.net

WINDY CITY OPEN DANCESPORT COMPETITION
Chicago, IL
Kris & Ella Kasperowicz, Glenn Weiss & Michelle Carpenter-Lazarz
TEL: (312) 409-3995 FAX: (509) 357-8770
Email: thewindycityopen@yahoo.com
http://www.thewindycityopen.com

EMBASSY BALL DANCESPORT CHAMPIONSHIPS, INC.
Irvine, CA
Brian & Kristi McDonald, Tetsuo Kezuko & Cheiko Yamamoto, John Kimmins & Sam Sodano
TEL: (909) 797 0801 FAX: (909) 797 0801
Email: TelSpin@aol.com
http://www.embassyball.com

UNITED STATES DANCE SPORT CHAMPIONSHIPS
Orlando, FL
American Ballroom Company
TEL: (310) 377-1847 FAX: (310) 541-7162
Email: abc@usdsc.com
http://www.usdsc.com

GALAXY DANCE FESTIVAL
Mesa, Arizona
Judy Nixon & Paul Jack
TEL: (623) 561-8229 / 640-9865 FAX: (623) 561-0829
Email: judynixon@aol.com
http://www.galaxy-dance.com

CLEVELAND DANCESPORT CHALLENGE
Cleveland, OH
Lisa & Nichy Vegas
TEL: (216) 292-7371 FAX: (216) 292-7381
Email: lisadans1@aol.com
http://www.clevelanddancesport.com

STARDUST OPEN
Atlantic City, NJ
Chuck Danza & Pete Taylor (DanceSport Inc.)
TEL: (267) 716-9905 FAX: (215) 561-6199
Email: stardustopen@gmail..com
http://www.stardustopen.com

FLORIDA'S FIRE AND ICE BALL
Tampa, FL
Gigi Farrell
TEL: (813) 323-0055 FAX: (813) 250-9218
Email: ggfarrelli@aol.com
http://www.fireandiceball.com

SOUTHWESTERN INVITATIONAL CHAMPIONSHIPS
Dallas, TX
David Kloss
TEL: 512-331-1083
Email: drkloss@sbcglobal.net
http://www.southwesterninvitational.com

HAWAII STAR BALL
Honolulu, HI
Hawaii Star Ball, Inc. (Geoffrey Fells)
TEL: (808) 955-3134 FAX: (808) 942-3852
Email: gmfells@msn.com
http://www.hawaiistarball.com

FIRST COAST CLASSIC DANCESPORT CHAMPIONSHIP
Jacksonville, FL
Julisar Enterprises, Inc. (Sarwat Kaluby)
TEL: (904) 338-9219
Email: SKaluby@aol.com
http://www.firstcoastclassic.com

CONSTITUTION STATE CHALLENGE DANCESPORT CHAMPIONSHIPS
Stamford, CT
Constitution State Challenge, Inc. (Ron Cote)
TEL: (860) 563-2623 FAX: (860) 529-5222
Email: mambo2341@aol.com
http://www.cscdancesport.com

GOLDEN STATE CHALLENGE
Orange County, CA
Richard and Jennifer Booth & Tom and Lori Hicks
TEL: (310) 544-8699 FAX: (310) 544-8699
Email: rbooth@boothdance.com

HOTLANTA DANCE CHALLENGE
Atlanta, GA
Eddie Ares & Nancy Senner
TEL: (404) 846-3201 FAX: (404) 254-1073
Email: areseddie@gmail.com

CHICAGO HARVEST MOON CHAMPIONSHIPS
Chicago, IL
Javier Jarquin
TEL: 773-685-8045/773-685-5415 FAX: (815) 723-4926
(May to December)
Email: tangofor2@sbcglobal.net

AUTUMN DANCE CLASSIC
San Francisco, CA
Gene Jennings
TEL: (415) 771-4748 FAX: (415) 771-4748
http://www.autumndanceclassic.com

NEW JERSEY STATE OPEN CHAMPIONSHIPS
Rutherford, NJ
American Star Productions, Inc. (Pete Taylor)
TEL: (302) 221-0331 FAX: (302) 221-0311
Email: info@crystaldansport.com
http://njopen.accessdance.com

GRAND NATIONAL DANCE FESTIVAL & CHAMPIONSHIPS
Miami Beach, FL
Dance America, Inc. (Peter & Cassandra Schneider)
TEL: (954) 227-1760 FAX: (954) 227-1761
Email: admin@grandnationalchampionship.com
http://www.grandnationalchampionship.com

COMMONWEALTH CLASSIC
Lowell, MA
Gail Rundlett
TEL: (617) 783-5467 / 921-7718 / 744-1818
FAX: (617) 926-6844
Email: gnrundlett@rcn.com
http://www.havetodance.com/commonwealthclassic

CARIBBEAN DANCESPORT CLASSIC & WORLD
PROFESSIONAL SALSA CHAMPIONSHIP
San Juan, Puerto Rico
Danny Villavicencio & Gary McDonald
TEL: (973) 810-3276 FAX: (973) 927-3590
Email: caribbeandansprt@aol.com
http://www.caribbeandancesport.com

PACIFIC DANCESPORT CHAMPIONSHIPS
Universal City, CA
Ali Marashi & Fidel Nabor
TEL: (425) 688-1010 FAX: (425) 688-7476
Email: pacificdance@yahoo.com
http://www.pacificdancesport.com

CAROLINA CLASSIC
Greensboro, NC
Patti Andersen Troy

TEL: (919) 736-3500 / Cell (941) 587-3277
FAX: (919) 735-3346
Email: pattitroy@earthlink.net
http://www.carolinaclassic.us

BRIGHAM YOUNG UNIVERSITY DANCESPORT
CHAMPIONSHIPS
Provo, UT
Curt Holman & Lee Wakefield
TEL: (801) 422-4623 FAX: (801) 422-0541
Email: Curt_Holman@byu.edu
http://www.byudancesport.com

OHIO STAR BALL BALLROOM CHAMPIONSHIPS
Columbus, OH
Sam Sodano
TEL: (614) 848-7827 FAX: (614) 847-5808
Email: OhStarBall@aol.com
http://www.ohiostarball.com

CALIFORNIA STAR BALL CHAMPIONSHIPS
Los Angeles, CA
John Morton & Gitte Svendsen
TEL: (661) 297-7257 FAX: (661) 297-7295
Email: Svendbgs@aol.com
http://www.californiastarball.com

SOUTHEASTERN STATES DANCE SPORT
CHAMPIONSHIPS
Orlando, FL
Dance Consultants, Unlimited Inc. (Larry &
Dianne Dean)
TEL: (888) 684-7717 / (941) 753-7940
FAX: (941) 753-7948
Email: deansofdance@aol.com
http://www.sestatesdance.com
E-mail address for Larry and Dianne Dean is: deansof-
dance@aol.com

YULETIDE BALL CHAMPIONSHIPS
Washington, DC
Ron Bennett
TEL: (301) 972-3271 FAX: (301) 972-3298
Email: Ronccbdcr@aol.com
http://www.yuletideball.com